MW01125083

I stand,
Thinking often,
Oh, that I might reach the other side.
-Teton

SKY PEOPLE, CREATURES & SPIRITS

FOLK TALES, LEGENDS AND PARANORMAL ENCOUNTERS OF THE FIRST NORTHERN AMERICANS

Compiled and Edited by
John E.L. Tenney

Photo Credits

Front Cover: Zahadolzha-Navajo; Page 12: A Navajo shaman;
Page 42: Giving the medicine-Navajo; Page 98: Haschebaad-Navajo;
Back Cover, Left: Gaaskidi - Navajo; Back Cover, Right: Haschezhini-Navajo

All photographs named above by Curtis, Edward S., 1868-1952, photographer.
Courtesy of Library of Congress,Washington, D.C. USA

Sky People, Creatures & Spirits
Folk Tales, Legends And Paranormal Encounters of The First Northern Americans

Second Edition
© 2013 John E.L. Tenney. All rights reserved.
ISBN 978-1490548555

Table of Contents

The Descending Star

One night a star shone strangely bright,
*   Out-shining all the rest.*
At first they deemed it far away,
*   Its nearness never guessed.*
Then some declared they believed it stood
*   Just over the tree-tops tall.*
To solve the doubt a council of
*   The wisest men they call.*

These went one night and found the star
*   Was something like a bird.*
It hovered just above the trees—
*   They feared, for they had heard*
From their forefathers that it might
*   A bloody war foretell,*
And over them a silent dread
*   Of some disaster fell.*

Chippewa legend

INTRODUCTION

I'm know that some readers of this volume will take issue with the fact that I have classified certain stories in this book as paranormal. To those readers I can only try to reinforce the idea that while our modern world has categorized these stories as "folk tales" or "morality plays," they still fall outside the realm of what we consider "normal." Just as the basis of every other culture's legends and myths have been lost to antiquity, so have the tales of the original inhabitants of North America. Who are we to say what is real and what is not?

As our knowledge of the universe increases with each scientific development and breakthrough, we have begun the process of quickly disregarding the stories of those who have come before us. We have never seen a man transform into a wolf, and indeed, science tells us it is an impossibility. Yet the underlying concept of "wild people," or humans that act in an animalistic manner, has simply been re-categorized under the heading of "mental illness."

The tales told by the original North Americans are some of the most colorful and curious you may stumble upon. With deep reflection, they allow the modern reader to speculate about the actual events which may have created the legends in the first place. Our society is rife with re-imaginings of ancient tales told by similar cultures. Many people believe that the ancient Egyptians were in contact with beings from outer space and that the South American Maya received their mathematics and astronomy from our space brethren. One thing is certain in the legends recounted in this book: The original inhabitants of North America had no issue educating their communities with the knowledge that "Sky People" did exist and very often interacted with the Earth's people.

When a person in our society weaves a fantastic tale of alien abduction or claims to have seen a flying object from another world, many may balk at the claims. But there are also those who wonder if there may be a scientific basis for the experience. I invite you to wonder, in the same manner, about the stories contained herein.

Not only does this book compile stories of spirits and unknown creatures, but it also reveals that some beliefs of people hundreds of years ago are not so different than those held by many today. As a specific example, in the community of modern people intrigued by paranormal phenomena, the concept of "Shadow Persons" is one that creates heated debates between its adherents. Yet "shadow people" were discussed and known to the Blackfeet centuries ago. They believed that a person's shadow was his or her soul and that if a person led a wicked life they were not allowed to move into the after-world and were confined to this world as wanderers envying the living and seeking to do harm. This is what many "paranormal researchers" still believe to this day. The more things change...

Sure, the ideas presented in these stories may be, and probably are, just the fanciful imaginative explanations of natural processes by people who did not have access to the scientific advancements we current have. At the same time, they are stories created by people who were more emotionally and psychologically in touch with their surrounding world. Our modern world is more technologically advanced - this is not doubted - but it is also filled with the endless errand running, bill paying and information overload that has separated us from the wondrous natural experiences of the planet that is our shared home. It was not a simpler time - your chances of being eaten by a bear have significantly decreased - but it was a time that allowed deeper introspective reflection.

No one can say for sure that the Thunder men of the Passamaquoddy were or were not extraterrestrial visitors. When a star or cloud containing people lowers itself from the sky, we can only wonder if the foundation of the story actually contained an unknown flying vehicle. If a great horned serpent appeared on the shore of California tomorrow it might be shocking, but we would classify, categorize, add it to our current knowledge base and move on to the next great discovery... unless the creature also spoke - that might shock and startle a few scientists.

There are endless documentaries and books about ancient extraterrestrials and their influence on humankind. The tales and legends of the original North Americans seem to have been pushed to the back of the crowd. Perhaps it is because they did not leave behind massive stone structures or pictograms that can only be seen from outer space, or maybe there is a more serious and embarrassing reason. The continent of North America was once populated by creative, beautiful people who saw themselves as children of the world, and they were systematically destroyed. As European and Latin cultures "discovered" a new world, they made sure that not only did the stories, cultures and gods of the original inhabitants vanish, but also the people themselves. This destruction of cultures, of course, did not happen 4,000 or 5,000 years ago, and the conquering people are not some long ago civilization that has also, since that time, vanished. It's easy to speculate on the legends and stories of the Sumerians; due to the antiquity of their culture, we have no real point of reference. But there can be many uncomfortable emotions when discussing the beliefs of a people that still exists, through their own tenacity and fortitude, after a recent attempt to purposefully vanish them from the face of the Earth.

As modern Americans, many of us spend vacations and weekends visiting buildings that are 100 or 200 years old. We desire a connection to an ancient history in such a degree that any object over a century in age tends to be kept behind glass and handed with the utmost care. We often forget the wondrous culture that is centuries old and happened in the rich forests that were cleared to build the residential neighborhoods we currently inhabit.

Here then are the memories, stories, and legends which persist. The tales that not only point out our similarities, but may also direct us to a large and more fascinating existence.

John E.L. Tenney
Winter 2014

Navajo Shaman: Circa 1890

SKY PEOPLE

THE CELESTIAL SISTERS

Waupee, or the White Hawk, lived in a remote part of the forest, where animals abounded. Every day he returned from the chase with a large spoil, for he was one of the most skillful and lucky hunters of his tribe. His form was like the cedar; the fire of youth beamed from his eye; there was no forest too gloomy for him to penetrate, and no track made by bird or beast of any kind which he could not readily follow.

One day he had gone beyond any point which he had ever before visited. He traveled through an open wood, which enabled him to see a great distance. At length he beheld a light breaking through the foliage of the distant trees, which made him sure that he was on the borders of a prairie. It was a wide plain, covered with long blue grass, and enameled with flowers of a thousand lovely tints.

After walking for some time without a path, musing upon the open country, and enjoying the fragrant breeze, he suddenly came to a ring worn among the grass and the flowers, as if it had been made by footsteps moving lightly round and round. But it was strange— so strange as to cause the White Hawk to pause and gaze long and fixedly upon the ground—there was no path which led to this flow-ery circle. There was not even a crushed leaf nor a broken twig, nor the least trace of a footstep, approaching or retiring, to be found. He thought he would hide himself and lie in wait to discover, if he could, what this strange circle meant.

Presently he heard the faint sounds of music in the air. He looked up in the direction they came from, and as the magic notes died away he saw a small object, like a little summer cloud that approaches the earth, floating down from above. At first it was very small, and seemed as if it could have been blown away by the first breeze that came along; but it rapidly grew as he gazed upon it, and the music every moment came clearer and more sweetly to his ear. As it neared the earth it appeared as a basket, and it was filled with twelve sisters, of the most lovely forms and enchanting beauty.

As soon as the basket touched the ground they leaped out, and began straightway to dance, in the most joyous manner, around the magic ring, striking, as they did so, a shining ball, which uttered the most ravishing melodies, and kept time as they danced.

The White Hawk, from his concealment, entranced, gazed upon their graceful forms and movements. He admired them all, but he was most pleased with the youngest. He longed to be at her side, to embrace her, to call her his own; and unable to remain longer a silent admirer, he rushed out and endeavored to seize this twelfth beauty who so enchanted him. But the sisters, with the quickness of birds, the moment they descried the form of a man, leaped back into the basket, and were drawn up into the sky.

Lamenting his ill-luck, Waupee gazed longingly upon the fairy basket as it ascended and bore the lovely sisters from his view. "They are gone," he said, "and I shall see them no more."

He returned to his solitary lodge, but he found no relief to his mind. He walked abroad, but to look at the sky, which had withdrawn from his sight the only being he had ever loved, was painful to him now.

The next day, selecting the same hour, the White Hawk went back to the prairie, and took his station near the ring; in order to deceive the sisters, he assumed the form of an opossum, and sat among the grass as if he were there engaged in chewing the cud. He had not waited long when he saw the cloudy basket descend, and heard the same sweet music falling as before. He crept slowly toward the ring; but the instant the sisters caught sight of him they were startled, and sprang into their car. It rose a short distance when one of the elder sisters spoke:

"Perhaps," she said, "it is come to show us how the game is played by mortals."

"Oh no," the youngest replied; "quick, let us ascend."

And all joining in a chant, they rose out of sight.

Waupee, casting off his disguise, walked sorrowfully back to his lodge—but ah, the night seemed very long to lonely White Hawk! His whole soul was filled with the thought of the beautiful sister.

Betimes, the next day, he returned to the haunted spot, hoping and fearing, and sighing as though his very soul would leave his body in its anguish. He reflected upon the plan he should follow to secure success. He had already failed twice; to fail a third time would be fatal. Near by he found an old stump, much covered with moss, and just then in use as the residence of a number of mice, who had stopped there on a pilgrimage to some relatives on the other side of the prairie. The White Hawk was so pleased with their tidy little forms that he thought he, too, would be a mouse, especially as they were by no means formidable to look at, and would not be at all likely to create alarm.

He accordingly, having first brought the stump and set it near the ring, without further notice became a mouse, and peeped and sported about, and kept his sharp little eyes busy with the others; but he did not forget to keep one eye up toward the sky, and one ear wide open in the same direction.

It was not long before the sisters, at their customary hour, came down and resumed their sport.

"But see," cried the younger sister, "that stump was not there before."

She ran off, frightened, toward the basket. Her sisters only smiled, and gathering round the old tree-stump, they struck it, in jest, when out ran the mice, and among them Waupee. They killed them all but one, which was pursued by the younger sister. Just as she had raised a silver stick which she held in her hand to put an end to it, too, the form of the White Hawk arose, and he clasped his prize in his arms. The other eleven sprang to their basket, and were drawn up to the skies.

Waupee exerted all his skill to please his bride and win her affections. He wiped the tears from her eyes; he related his adventures in the chase; he dwelt upon the charms of life on the earth. He was constant in his attentions, keeping fondly by her side, and picking out the way for her to walk as he led her gently toward his lodge. He felt his heart glow with joy as he entered it, and from that moment he was one of the happiest of men.

Winter and summer passed rapidly away, and as the spring drew near with its balmy gales and its many-colored flowers, their happiness was increased by the presence of a beautiful boy in their lodge. What more of earthly blessing was there for them to enjoy?

Waupee's wife was a daughter of one of the stars; and as the scenes of earth began to pall upon her sight, she sighed to revisit her father. But she was obliged to hide these feelings from her husband. She remembered the charm that would carry her up, and while White Hawk was engaged in the chase, she took occasion to construct a wicker basket, which she kept concealed. In the mean time, she collected such rarities from the earth as she thought would please her father, as well as the most dainty kinds of food.

One day when Waupee was absent, and all was in readiness, she went out to the charmed ring, taking with her her little son. As they entered the car she commenced her magical song, and the basket rose. The song was sad, and of a lowly and mournful cadence, and as it was wafted far away by the wind, it caught her husband's ear. It was a voice which he well knew, and he instantly ran to the prairie. Though he made breathless speed, he could not reach the ring before his wife and child had ascended beyond his reach. He lifted up his voice in loud appeals, but they were unavailing. The basket still went up. He watched it till it became a small speck, and finally it vanished in the sky. He then bent his head down to the ground, and was miserable.

Through a long winter and a long summer Waupee bewailed his loss, but he found no relief. The beautiful spirit had come and gone, and he should see it no more!

He mourned his wife's loss sorely, but his son's still more; for the boy had both the mother's beauty and the father's strength.

In the mean time his wife had reached her home in the stars, and in the blissful employments of her father's house she had almost forgotten that she had left a husband upon the earth. But her son, as he grew up, resembled more and more his father, and every day he was restless and anxious to visit the scene of his birth. His grandfather said to his daughter, one day:

"Go, my child, and take your son down to his father, and ask him to come up and live with us. But tell him to bring along a specimen of each kind of bird and animal he kills in the chase."

She accordingly took the boy and descended The White Hawk, who was ever near the enchanted spot, heard her voice as she came down the sky. His heart beat with impatience as he saw her form and that of his son, and they were soon clasped in his arms.

He heard the message of the Star, and he began to hunt with the greatest activity, that he might collect the present with all dispatch. He spent whole nights, as well as days, in searching for every curious and beautiful animal and bird. He only preserved a foot, a wing, or a tail of each.

When all was ready, Waupee visited once more each favorite spot— the hill-top whence he had been used to see the rising sun; the stream where he had sported as a boy; the old lodge, now looking sad and solemn, which he was to sit in no more; and last of all, coming to the magic circle, he gazed widely around him with tearful eyes, and, taking his wife and child by the hand, they entered the car and were drawn up—into a country far beyond the flight of birds, or the power of mortal eye to pierce.

Great joy was manifested upon their arrival at the starry plains. The Star Chief invited all his people to a feast; and when they had assembled, he proclaimed aloud that each one might continue as he was, an inhabitant of his own dominions, or select of the earthly gifts such as he liked best. A very strange confusion immediately arose; not one but sprang forward. Some chose a foot, some a wing, some a tail, and some a claw. Those who selected tails or claws were changed into animals, and ran off; the others assumed the form of birds, and flew away. Waupee chose a White Hawk's feather. His wife and son followed his example, and each one became a white hawk. He spread his wings, and, followed by his wife and son, descended with the other birds to the earth, where he is still to be found, with the brightness of the starry plains in his eye, and the freedom of the heavenly breezes in his wings.

TWIN CHILDREN OF THE SUN

"Long ago there were great monsters on this earth. Some of them were enormous animals and fiercer than any that now exist. Then there were magicians, and other evil spirits, like windegoos, some of whom were tall, giant cannibals, that filled the people with terror. They lay in wait and caught the children, and even the grown-up people, as the wild beasts now catch their prey. Then they kindled up great fires and roasted them and ate them.

"Often, when the parents went to look for their children, they also were caught and eaten.

"The people were rendered very miserable not only by these great monsters in human form, but also by the attacks of the enormous animals that then lived. Indeed they began to fear that they would all soon be killed, unless help came to them.

These people were worshipers of the sun, whom they called the great Sun Father, and some tribes still have their sun dances in his honor. When he saw that the people were in such great trouble and were likely to be all killed by their cruel enemies he resolved to deliver them from their foes. So he disguised himself and came down to the earth and married a beautiful woman of the Northland. They had lovely twin boys, whose names were Sesigizit, the older, and Ooseemeeid, the younger. (Algonquin)

THE FALLEN STAR

There were two women sleeping out of doors and looking up at the stars.

One of them said, "I wish that that large and bright shining star were my husband."

The other said, "I wish the star that shines less brightly were my husband."

And immediately both were immediately carried upward, they say. They found themselves in a beautiful country which was full of beautiful twin flowers. And they found that the star which had shone most brightly was a large man; the other star was only a young man. So the two stars married the two women and they lived in that beautiful Star Country.

Now in that country was a plant, the Teepsinna, with large, attractive stalks. The wife of the large star wanted to dig them. Her husband said, "No; no one does so here."

Then the camp moved. When the woman had pitched her tepee, and came inside to lay the mats, she saw there a beautiful Teepsinna. She said to herself, "I will dig this; no one will see me." So she took her digging stick and dug the teepsinna; but when she pulled it out of the earth, the foundation of the Star Country broke and she fell through with her baby. So the woman died; but the baby was not injured. It lay there stretched out.

An old man came that way. When he saw that the baby was alive, he took it in his blanket and took it to his own lodge. He said to his wife, "Old woman, I saw something today that made my heart feel badly."

"What was it?" she asked.

"A woman lay dead; and a little baby boy lay beside her kicking."

"Why did you not bring it home, old man?" she asked.

"Here it is," he said. Then he took it out of his blanket.

The wife said, "Old man, let us adopt this child."

The old man said, "We will swing it around the tepee." He whirled it up through the smoke hole. It went whirling around and around and fell down, and came creeping into the tent.

Again he took up the baby and threw it up through the smoke hole. It got up and came into the tent walking. Again the old man whirled him out. In came a boy with some green sticks. He said, "Grandfather, I wish you would make me arrows."

Again the old man whirled him out. No one knows where he went. This time he came back into the tepee a long man, with many green sticks. He said, "Grandfather, make me arrows of these."

So the old man made him arrows, and he killed a great many buffaloes, and they made a large tepee, and built up a high sleeping place in the back part of the tepee, and were very rich in dried meat.

The old man said, "Old woman, I am glad we are well off; I will proclaim it abroad." So when morning came, he went to the top of the tent, and sat, and said, "I, I have abundance laid up. I eat the fat of the animals."

That is how the meadow lark came to be made, they say. It has a yellow breast and black in the middle, which is the yellow of that morning, and they say the black stripe is made by a smooth buffalo horn worn for a necklace.

The young man said, "Grandfather, I want to go visiting."

"Yes," said the old man. "When one is young is the time to go visiting."

The young man went and came to a people, and lo! they were engaged in shooting arrows through a hoop. And there was a young man who was simply looking on. By and by he said, "My friend, let us go to your house."

So they came to his lodge. Now this young man also had been raised by his grandmother, and lived with her, they say.

"Grandmother, I have brought my friend home with me; get him something to eat," said the grandson.

Grandmother said, "What shall I do?"

Then the visiting young man said, "How is it, grandmother?"

She said, "The people are about to die of thirst. All who go for water will not come back again."

Fallen Star said, "My friend, take a kettle; we will go for water."

"With difficulty have I raised my grandchild," objected the old woman.

"You are afraid of trifles," said the grandson. So he went with Star-born.

They reached the side of the lake. By the water of the lake stood troughs half full of water.

Star-born called out, "You who they say have killed every one who has come for water, where have you gone? I have come for water."

Then immediately whither they went is not manifest. Behold, there was a long house which was extended, and it was full of young men and women. Some of them were dead and some were dying.

"How did you come here?" asked Star-born.

They replied, "What do you mean? We came for water and something swallowed us."

Something kept striking on the head of Star-born.

"What is this?" he said.

"Get away," they replied, "that is the heart."

Then he drew out his knife and cut it to pieces. Suddenly something made a great noise. In the great body, these people were swallowed up. When the heart died, death came to the body. Then Star-born cut a great hole in the side, and came out, bringing the young men and the young women. All came to life again.

So the people were thankful and offered him two wives.

But he said, "I am journeying. My friend here will marry them."

Then Star-born went on, they say. Again he found a young man standing where they were shooting through a hoop. He said, "I will look on with my friend," and went and stood beside him.

Then the other said, "My friend, let us go home," so he went with him to his tepee.

"Grandmother, I have brought my friend home with me," he said. "Get him something to eat."

Grandmother replied, "How shall I do as you say?"

"How is it?" said Star-born.

"This people are perishing for wood," she said; "when any one goes for wood, he never comes home again."

Star-born said, "My friend, take the packing strap; we will go for wood."

The old woman protested. "This one, my grandchild, I have raised with difficulty," she said. He answered, "Old woman, what you are afraid of are trifles," and went with the young man. "I am going to bring wood," he said. "If any wish to go, come along."

"The young man who came from somewhere says this," they said, so they followed him.

They had now reached the wood. They found it tied up in bundles. He ordered them to carry it home, but he stood still and said, "You who killed every one who came to this wood, where have you gone?"

Then, suddenly, where he went was not made manifest. And lo! a te-pee, and in it some young men and young women; some were eating, and some were waiting.

He said to them, "How came you here?"

They answered, "What do you mean? We came for wood and some-thing brought us here. Now you also are lost."

He looked behind him, and lo! there was a hole.

"What is this?" he asked.

"Stop!" they said. "That is the thing itself."

He drew out an arrow and shot it. Then suddenly it opened out and behold! it was the ear of an owl in which they had been shut up. When it was killed, it opened out. Then he said, "Young men and women, come out," so they went home.

Again they offered him two wives. But he said, "My friend will marry them. I am traveling."

Again he passed on. And he came to a dwelling place of people and found them shooting the hoop. There stood a young man looking on. He joined him as his friend. While they stood there together, he said:

"Friend, let us go to your home." So he went with him to his tepee.

The young man said, "Grandmother, I have brought my friend home with me; get him something to eat."

She said, "Where shall I get it from, that you say that?"

"Grandmother, how is it that you say so?" asked the stranger.

She replied, "Waziya treats this people very badly. When they go out to kill buffalo, he takes it all, and now they are starving to death."

Now Waziya was a giant who caused very cold weather and blizzards.

Then he said, "Grandmother, go to him and say, 'My grandchild has come on a journey and has nothing to eat; so he has sent me to you.'"

So the old woman went and standing at a distance, cried, "Waziya, my grandchild has come on a journey and has nothing to eat; so he has sent me to you."

He replied, "Bad old woman, get you home; what do you mean by coming here?"

The old woman came home crying, and saying that Waziya had threatened to kill some of her relations.

Star-born said, "My friend, take your strap; we will go there."

The old woman interfered: "I have with difficulty raised my grandchild."

Grandchild replied to this by saying, "Grandmother is very much afraid." So the two went together.

When they came to the house of Waziya, they found a great deal of dried meat outside. He put as much on his friend as he could carry, and sent him home with it; then Star-born entered the tepee of Waziya, and said to him, "Waziya, why did you answer my grandmother as you did when I sent her to you?"

Waziya only looked angry.

Hanging there was a bow of ice. "Waziya, why do you keep this?" he said.

The giant replied, "Hands off; whoever touches that gets a broken arm."

Star-born said, "I will see if my arm breaks." He took the ice bow and snapped it into many pieces, and then started home.

The next morning all the people went on the chase and killed many buffaloes. But, as he had done before, the Waziya went all over the field, gathered up all the meat, and put it in his blanket.

Star-born was cutting up a fat cow. Waziya came and stood there. He said, "Who cuts this up?"

"I am," answered Star-born.

Waziya said, "From where have you come that you act so haughtily?"

"Whence have you come, Waziya, that you act so proudly?" he retorted.

Waziya said, "Fallen Star, whoever points his finger at me dies." The young man thought, "I will point my finger at him and see if I die." He pointed his finger, but it made no difference.

Then Fallen Star said, "Waziya, whoever points his finger at me, his hand loses all use." So Waziya thought, "I will point my finger and see." He pointed his finger. His forearm lost all use. Then he pointed his finger with the other hand. It was destroyed even to the elbow.

Then Fallen Star drew out his knife and cut up Waziya's blanket, and all the buffalo meat he had gathered there fell out. Fallen Star called to the people, "Henceforth kill and carry home."

So the people took the meat and carried it to their tepees.

The next morning, they say, it was rumored that the blanket of Waziya, which had been cut to pieces, had been sewed up by his wife. He was about to shake it.

The giant stood with his face toward the north and shook his blanket. Then the wind blew from the north. Snow fell all about the camp so that the people were all snowed in. They were much troubled. They said, "We did live in some fashion before; but now this young man has acted so we are in great trouble."

But he said, "Grandmother, find me a fan."

Then she made a road under the snow, and went to people and said, "My grandchild says he wants a fan."

"What does he mean by saying that?" they asked and gave him one.

Now the snow reached to the top of the lodges, and so Fallen Star pushed up through the snow, and sat on the ridge of the lodge. While the wind was blowing to the south, he sat and fanned himself and made the wind come from the south. Then the heat became great. The snow went as if boiling water had been poured over it. All over the ground there was a mist. Waziya and his wife and children all died with the great heat. But the youngest child, the littlest child of Waziya, took refuge in the hole made by the tent pole, where there was a frost, and so he lived. So they say that is all that is left of Waziya now, just the littlest child.

(Dakota)

OLD-WOMAN-WHO-NEVER-DIES

In the sun lives the Lord of Life. In the moon lives Old-Woman-Who-Never-Dies. She has six children, three sons and three daughters. These live in the sky. The eldest son is the Day; another is the Sun; another is Night. The eldest daughter is the Morning Star, called "The Woman who Wears a Plume"; another is a star which circles around the polar star, and she is called "The Striped Gourd"; the third is Evening Star.

Every spring Old-Woman-Who-Never-Dies sends the wild geese, the swans, and the ducks. When she sends the wild geese, the Indians plant their corn and Old-Woman-Who-Never-Dies makes it grow. When eleven wild geese are found together, the Indians know the corn crop will be very large. The swans mean that the Indians must plant gourds; the ducks, that they must plant beans.

Indians always save dried meat for these wild birds, so when they come in the spring they may have a corn feast. They build scaffolds of many poles, three or four rows, and one above the others. On this they hang the meat. Then the old women in the village, each one with a stick, meet around the scaffold. In one end of the stick is an ear of corn. Sitting in a circle, they plant their sticks in the ground in front of them. Then they dance around the scaffolds while the old men beat the drums and rattle the gourds.

Afterwards the old women in the village are allowed to eat the dried meat.

In the fall they hold another corn feast, after the corn is ripe. This is so that Old-Woman-Who-Never-Dies may send the buffalo herds to them. Each woman carries the entire cornstalk, with the ears attached, just as it was pulled up by the roots. Then they call on Old-Woman-Who-Never-Dies and say,

"Mother, pity us. Do not send the cold too soon, or we may not have enough meat. Mother, do not let the game depart, so that we may have enough for winter."

In the fall, when the birds go south to Old-Woman, they take back the dried meat hung on the scaffolds, because Old-Woman is very fond of it.

Old-Woman-Who-Never-Dies has large patches of corn, kept for her by the great stag and by the white-tailed stag. Blackbirds also help her guard her corn patches. The corn patches are large, therefore the Old Woman has the help also of the mice and the moles. In the spring the birds go north, back to Old-Man-Who-Never-Dies.

In the olden time, Old-Woman-Who-Never-Dies lived near the Little Missouri. Sometimes the Indians visited her. One day twelve came, and she offered them only a small kettle of corn. They were very hungry and the kettle was very small. But as soon as it was empty, it at once became filled again, so all the Indians had enough to eat.

(Mandan)

THE MOON AND THE GREAT SNAKE

The rain had passed; the moon looked down from a clear sky, and the bushes and dead grass smelled wet, after the heavy storm. A cottontail ran into a clump of wild-rose bushes near War Eagle's lodge, and some dogs were close behind the frightened animal, as he gained cover. Little Buffalo Calf threw a stone into the bushes, scaring the rabbit from his hiding-place, and away went bunny, followed by the yelping pack. We stood and listened until the noise of the chase died away, and then went into the lodge, where we were greeted, as usual, by War Eagle. To-night he smoked; but with greater ceremony, and I suspected that it had something to do with the forthcoming story. Finally he said:

"You have seen many Snakes, I suppose?"

"Yes," replied the children, "we have seen a great many. In the summer we see them every day."

"Well," continued the story-teller, "once there was only one Snake on the whole world, and he was a big one, I tell you. He was pretty to look at, and was painted with all the colors we know. This snake was proud of his clothes and had a wicked heart. Most Snakes are wicked, because they are his relations.

"Now, I have not told you all about it yet, nor will I tell you to-night, but the Moon is the Sun's wife, and some day I shall tell you that story, but to-night I am telling you about the Snakes.

"You know that the Sun goes early to bed, and that the Moon most always leaves before he gets to the lodge. Sometimes this is not so, but that is part of another story.

"This big Snake used to crawl up a high hill and watch the Moon in the sky. He was in love with her, and she knew it; but she paid no attention to him. She liked his looks, for his clothes were fine, and he was always slick and smooth. This went on for a long time, but she never talked to him at all. The Snake thought maybe the hill wasn't high enough, so he found a higher one, and watched the Moon pass, from the top. Every night he climbed this high hill and motioned to her. She began to pay more attention to the big Snake, and one morning early, she loafed at her work a little, and spoke to him. He was flattered, and so was she, because he said many nice things to her, but she went on to the Sun's lodge, and left the Snake.

"The next morning very early she saw the Snake again, and this time she stopped a long time—so long that the Sun had started out from the lodge before she reached home. He wondered what kept her so long, and became suspicious of the Snake. He made up his mind to watch, and try to catch them together. So every morning the Sun left the lodge a little earlier than before; and one morning, just as he climbed a mountain, he saw the big Snake talking to the Moon. That made him angry, and you can't blame him, because his wife was spending her time loafing with a Snake.

"She ran away; ran to the Sun's lodge and left the Snake on the hill. In no time the Sun had grabbed him. My, the Sun was angry! The big Snake begged, and promised never to speak to the Moon again, but the Sun had him; and he smashed him into thousands of little pieces, all of different colors from the different parts of his painted body. The little pieces each turned into a little snake, just as you see them now, but they were all too small for the Moon to notice after that. That is how so many Snakes came into the world; and that is why they are all small, nowadays.

"Our people do not like the Snake-people very well, but we know that they were made to do something on this world, and that they do it, or they wouldn't live here.

THE ORPHAN BOY AND THE MOON

"Long ago, there was a poor orphan boy who had neither father nor mother, uncle, aunt, nor any living relative that he knew of. He had a very hard time of it, as the people did not seem to take kindly to him. So he had to live just where he could. He managed to get along all right during the pleasant summer time, but when the long cold winters began he suffered very much. One winter some selfish people let him live with them because he was willing to work hard for what little they did for him. They treated him badly in many ways. They made him go out into the woods and cut firewood, but when he brought it home they would only allow him to stay in the cold entry-way which they had built to their winter dwelling.

"They made him go and hunt different animals for food, and then when he brought, them home they cooked and ate the best themselves, and just threw the fragments and bones to him as they would to a dog. Every member of the household treated him very cruelly, except a nice little girl, the youngest daughter of the family. She felt very sorry for him. She would secretly take him better food, and she furnished him with a knife with which he could cut the tough pieces of meat. She had to be very careful not to be discovered, for if found out she would have been severely punished. So her pity had to show itself on the sly, and the few words she was able to tell him of her sympathy had to be whispered as she passed him, when nobody was looking or listening. The poor boy up to this time had no ambition to better himself, but her kind words and deeds made him resolve that he must begin and do something for himself. But what could he do? Everybody seemed against him but this little girl, and she could do nothing in the way of helping him to escape from these people, who, now that he was becoming so useful to them, would not let him go. What, really, could he do?

"Thus the days and weeks and months passed on and there seemed no chance of escape. He had tried to run away, but had been caught and brought back and beaten.

THE LONE LIGHTNING

A little orphan boy, who had no one to care for him, once lived with his uncle, who treated him very badly, making him do hard work, and giving him very little to eat, so that the boy pined away and never grew much, but became, through hard usage, very thin and light. At last the uncle pretended to be ashamed of this treatment, and determined to make amends for it by fattening the boy up. He really wished, however, to kill him by overfeeding him. He told his wife to give the boy plenty of bear's meat, and let him have the fat, which is thought to be the best part. They were both very assiduous in cramming him, and one day nearly choked him to death by forcing the fat down his throat. The boy escaped, and fled from the lodge. He knew not where to go, and wandered about. When night came on he was afraid the wild beasts would eat him, so he climbed up into the forks of a high pine-tree, and there he fell asleep in the branches.

As he was asleep a person appeared to him from the high sky, and said—

"My poor lad, I pity you, and the bad usage you have received from your uncle has led me to visit you. Follow me, and step in my tracks."

Immediately his sleep left him, and he rose up and followed his guide, mounting up higher and higher in the air until he reached the lofty sky. Here twelve arrows were put into his hands, and he was told that there were a great many manitoes in the northern sky, against whom he must go to war and try to waylay and shoot them. Accordingly he went to that part of the sky, and, at long intervals, shot arrow after arrow until he had expended eleven in a vain attempt to kill the manitoes. At the flight of each arrow there was a long and solitary streak of lightning in the sky—then all was clear again, and not a cloud or spot could be seen. The twelfth arrow he held a long time in his hands, and looked around keenly on every side to spy the manitoes he was after, but these manitoes were very cunning, and could change their form in a moment. All they feared was the boy's arrows, for these were magic weapons, which had been given to him by a good spirit, and had power to kill if aimed aright. At length the boy drew up his last arrow, took aim, and let fly, as he thought, into the very heart of the chief of the manitoes. Before the arrow reached him, however, he changed himself into a rock, into which the head of the arrow sank deep and stuck fast.

"Now your gifts are all expended," cried the enraged manito, "and I will make an example of your audacity and pride of heart for lifting your bow against me."

So saying, he transformed the boy into the Nazhik-a-wä wä sun, or Lone Lightning, which may be observed in the northern sky to this day.

"One night when it was not very cold he went outside of the narrow entry where he generally had to sleep and threw himself on the ground and cried in his sorrow and despair. He seemed to be utterly unable to better himself. As he lay there he began looking up at the great bright moon that, now so large and round, was, he thought, looking earnestly at him. Soon he was able to see that there was a great man in the moon. As he watched him he was glad to notice that he was not looking crossly at him, but kindly, and so he began crying to the man in the moon to come and help him to escape from the miserable life he was leading. Sure enough, as the boy kept on crying and pleading he saw the man in the moon beginning to come down to this world. He came to the very spot where the unhappy boy was lying, but instead of helping him he made him stand up and then he gave him a good sound thrashing, making the boy, however, strike back at him as vigorously as he could. The beating he got very much disheartened and discouraged the boy, for it was not what he had expected. On the following night, when he had recovered a little, he began reproaching the man in the moon.

"'I called for you,' he said, 'to come and help me against my enemies, and now you have come and thrashed me.'

"But these words, instead of softening the man in the moon, caused him to come down again and give the poor boy a far worse thrashing than before, but for every blow he made the boy return one as good as he had received.

"Now for the first time the boy began to notice that the more he was beaten the stronger he grew. Still he could not understand what the man in the moon meant. So he came again, and they had another regular set-to, and the boy had another good sound thrashing. He asked him what was the meaning of his beating him thus. The man in the moon now spoke to him, but his words were so much like a puzzle that at first the boy did not understand them. This is what the man in the moon said:

'Would you triumph o'er the strong?
Be strong.
Would you let them no more conquer?
Conquer.'

"For a time the boy repeated them over and over. He used to say that as the result of these meetings with the man in the moon he had grown so strong that he was nearly able to hold his own against his

SKY PEOPLE, CREATURES & SPIRITS

antagonist. Then one day, when the man in the moon was puffing from the encounter, the latter said:

"'Now by hard knocks and exercise I have put you on the way of ending your troubles. Be strong, and conquer. Farewell! I am not coming again, as you do not need me anymore.'

"Then away he flew back to his place in the moon.

ONAIAZO, THE SKY-WALKER

A long time ago, there lived an aged Odjibwa and his wife, on the Shores of Lake Huron. They had an only son, a very beautiful boy, whose name was O-na-wut-a-qut-o, or He-That-Catches-Clouds. The family were of the totem of the beaver. The parents were very proud of him, and thought to make him a celebrated man, but when he reached the proper age, he would not submit to the We-koon-de-win, or fast. When this time arrived, they gave him charcoal, instead of his breakfast, but he would not blacken his face. If they denied him food, he would seek for birds' eggs, along the shores, or pick up the heads of fish that had been cast away, and broil them. One day, they took away violently the food he had thus prepared, and cast him some coals in place of it. This act brought him to a decision. He took the coals and blackened his face, and went out of the lodge. He did not return, but slept without; and during the night, he had a dream. He dreamed that he saw a very beautiful female come down from the clouds and stand by his side. "O-no-wut-a-qut-o," said she, "I am come for you—step in my tracks." The young man did so, and presently felt himself ascending above the tops of the trees—he mounted up, step by step, into the air, and through the clouds. His guide, at length, passed through an orifice, and he, following her, found himself standing on a beautiful plain.

A path led to a splendid lodge. He followed her into it. It was large, and divided into two parts. On one end he saw bows and arrows, clubs and spears, and various warlike implements tipped with silver. On the other end were things exclusively belonging to females. This was the home of his fair guide, and he saw that she had, on the frame, a broad rich belt, of many colors, which she was weaving. She said to him: "My brother is coming and I must hide you." Putting him in one corner, she spread the belt over him. Presently the brother came in, very richly dressed, and shining as if he had points of silver all over him. He took down from the wall a splendid pipe, together with his sack of a-pa-ko-ze-gun, or smoking mixture. When he had finished regaling himself in this way, and laid his pipe aside, he said to his sister: "Nemissa, when will you quit these practices? Do you forget that the Greatest of the Spirits had commanded that you should not take away the child from below? Perhaps you suppose that you have concealed O-no-wut-a-qut-o, but do I not know of his coming? If you would not offend me, send him back immediately." But this address did not alter her purpose. She would not send him back. Finding that she was purposed in her mind, he then spoke to the young lad, and called him from his hiding-place. "Come out of your concealment," said he, "and walk about and amuse yourself. You will grow hungry if you remain there." He then presented him a bow and arrows, and a pipe of red stone, richly ornamented. This was taken as the word of consent to his marriage; so the two were considered husband and wife from that time.

O-no-wut-a-qut-o found everything exceedingly fair and beautiful around him, but he found no inhabitants except her brother. There were flowers on the plains. There were bright and sparkling streams. There were green valleys and pleasant trees. There were gay birds and beautiful animals, but they were not such as he had been accustomed to see. There was also day and night, as on the earth; but he observed that every morning the brother regularly left the lodge, and remained absent all day; and every evening the sister departed, though it was commonly but for a part of the night.

His curiosity was aroused to solve this mystery. He obtained the brother's consent to accompany him in one of his daily journeys. They travelled over a smooth plain, without boundaries, until O-no-wut-a-qut-o felt the gnawings of appetite, and asked his companion if there were no game. "Patience! my brother," said he, "we shall soon reach the spot where I eat my dinner, and you will then see how I am provided." After walking on a long time, they came to a place which was spread over with fine mats, where they sat down to refresh themselves. There was, at this place, a hole through the sky; and O-no-wut-a-qut-o, looked down, at the bidding of his companion, upon the earth. He saw below the great lakes, and the villages of the Indians. In one place, he saw a war party stealing on the camp of their enemies. In another, he saw feasting and dancing. On a green plain, young men were engaged at ball. Along a stream, women were employed in gathering the a-puk-wa for mats.

"Do you see," said the brother, "that group of children playing beside a lodge? Observe that beautiful and active boy," said he, at the same time darting something at him, from his hand. The child immediately fell, and was carried into the lodge.

They looked again, and saw the people gathering about the lodge. They heard the she-she-gwun, of the meeta, and the song he sung, asking that the child's life might be spared. To this request, the companion of O-no-wut-a-qut-o made answer: "Send me up the sacrifice of a white deer." Immediately a feast was ordered by the parents of the child, the white deer was killed, his carcass was roasted, and all the wise men and medicine men of the village assembled to witness the ceremony. "There are many below," continued the voice of the brother, "whom you call great in medical skill, but it is because their ears are open, and they listen to my voice, that they are able to succeed. When I have struck one with sickness, they direct the people to look to me; and when they send me the offering I ask, I remove my hand from off them, and they are well." After he had said this, they saw the sacrifice parcelled out in dishes, for those who were at the feast. The master of the feast then said, "We send this to thee, great Manito," and immediately the roasted animal came up. Thus their dinner was supplied, and after they had eaten, they returned to the lodge by another way.

After this manner they lived for some time; but the place became wearisome at last. O-no-wut-a-qut-o thought of his friends, and wished to go back to them. He had not forgotten his native village, and his father's lodge; and he asked leave of his wife to return. At length she consented. "Since you are better pleased," she replied, "with the cares and the ills, and the poverty of the world, than with the peaceful delights of the sky, and its boundless prairies, go! I give you permission, and since I have brought you hither, I will conduct you back; but, remember, you are still my husband, I hold a chain in my hand by which I can draw you back whenever I will. My power over you is not, in any manner, diminished. Beware, therefore, how you venture to take a wife among the people below. Should you ever do so, it is then that you shall feel the force of my displeasure."

As she said this, her eyes sparkled—she raised herself slightly on her toes, and stretched herself up, with a majestic air; and at that moment, O-no-wut-a-qut-o awoke from his dream. He found himself on the ground, near his father's lodge, at the very spot where he had laid himself down to fast. Instead of the bright beings of a higher world, he found himself surrounded by his parents and relatives. His mother told him he had been absent a year. The change was so great, that he remained for some time moody and abstracted, but by degrees he recovered his spirits. He began to doubt the reality of all he had heard and seen above. At last, he forgot the admonitions of his spouse, and married a beautiful young woman of his own tribe. But within four days, she was a corpse. Even this fearful admonition was lost, and he repeated the offence by a second marriage. Soon afterwards, he went out of the lodge, one night, but never returned. It was believed that his Sun-wife had recalled him to the region of the clouds, where, the tradition asserts, he still dwells, and walks on the daily rounds, which he once witnessed.

(Ottawa)

A VISIT TO THE THUNDER SPIRITS

Once an Indian went forth to hunt. And he departed from the east branch of the Penobscot, and came to the head of another branch that leads into the east branch, and this he followed even to the foot of Mount Katahdin. And there he hunted many a day alone, and met none, till one morning in midwinter he found the track of snow-shoes. So he returned to his camp; but the next day he met with it again in a far-distant place. And thus it was that, wherever he went, this track came to him every day. Then noting this, as a sign to be observed, he followed it, and it went up the mountain, Katahdin, which, being interpreted, means "the great mountain," until at last it was lost in a hard snow-shoe road made by many travelers. And since it was hard and even, he took off his agahmook, or snow-shoes, and went ever on and up with the road; and it was a strange path and strange was its ending, for it stopped just before a high ledge, like an immense wall, on a platform at its foot. And there were many signs there, as of many people, yet he saw no one. And as he stayed it seemed to grow stranger and stranger. At last he heard a sound as of footsteps coming, yet within the wall, when lo! a girl stepped directly out of the precipice upon the platform. But though she was beautiful beyond belief, he was afraid. And to his every thought she answered in words, and that so sweetly and kindly and cleverly that he was soon without fear, though he saw that she had powerful m'teoulin, or great magic power. And they being soon pleased one with the other, and wanting each other, she bade him accompany her, and that by walking directly through the rock. "Have no fear," said she, "but, advance boldly!" So he obeyed, and lo! the rock was as the air, and it gave way as he went on. And ever as they went the maiden talked to him, answering his thoughts, so that he spoke not aloud.

They came to a great cavern far within, and there was an old man seated by a fire, and the old man welcomed him. And he was very kindly treated by the strange pair all day: in all his life he had never been so happy. Now as the night drew near, the old man said to his daughter, "Can you hear aught of your brothers?" Then she went out to the terrace, and, returning, said, "No." Then he asked her again, and she, going and returning as before, replied, "Now I hear them coming." Then they listened, when lo! there came, as at the door without, a crash of thunder with a flash of lightning, and out of the light stepped two young men of great beauty, but like giants, stupendous and awful men. And, like their father, their eyebrows were of stone, while their cheeks were as rocks.

And the hunter was told by their sister that when they went forth, which was every few days, their father said to them, "Sons, arise! it is time now for you to go forth over the world and save our friends. Go not too near the trees, but if you see aught that is harmful to those whom we love, strike, and spare not!" Then when they went forth they flew on high among the clouds; and thus it is that the Thunder and Lightning, whose home is in the mighty Katahdin, are made. And when the thunder strikes, the brothers are shooting at the enemies of their friends.

Now when the day was done the hunter returned to his home, and when there, found he had been gone seven years. All this I have heard from the old people who are dead and gone.

(Passamaquoddy)

THE THUNDER AND LIGHTNING MEN

Once an Indian was whirled up by the roaring wind: he was taken up in a thunder-storm, and set down again in the village of the Thunders. In after-times he described them as very like human beings: they used bows and arrows but also had wings.

Their wings can be laid aside, and kept for use. And from time to time their chief gives these Thunders orders to put them on, and tells them where to go. He also tells them how long they are to be gone, and warns them not to go too low, for it is sure death for them to be caught in the crotch of a tree.

The great chief of the Thunders, hearing of the stranger's arrival, sent for him, and received him very kindly, and told him that he would do well to become one of them. To which the man being willing, the chief soon after called all his people together to see the ceremony of thunderifying the Indian.

Then they bade him go into a strange square box, and while in it he lost his senses and became a Thunder. Then they brought him a pair of wings, and he put them on. So he flew about like the rest of the Thunders; he became quite like them, and followed all their ways. And he said that they always flew towards the south, and that the roar and crash of the thunder was the sound of their wings. Their great amusement is to play at ball across the sky. When they return they carefully put away their wings for their next flight. There is a big bird in the south, and this they are always trying to kill, but never succeed in doing so.

They made long journeys, and always took him with them. So it went on for a long time, but it came to pass that the Indian began to tire of his strange friends. Then he told the chief that he wished to see his family on earth, and the sagamore listened to him and was very kind. Then he called all his people together, and said that their brother from the other world was very lonesome, and wished to return. They were all very sorry indeed to lose him, but because they loved him they let him have his own way, and decided to carry him back again. So bidding him close his eyes till he should be on earth, they carried him down.

The Indians saw a great thunder-storm drawing near; they heard such thunder as they never knew before, and then something in the shape of a human being coming down with lightning; then they ran to the spot where he sat, and it was their long-lost brother, who had been gone seven years.

He had been in the Thunder-world. He told them how he had been playing ball with the Thunder-boys and how he had been turned into a real Thunder himself.

(Passamaquoddy)

THE CLOUD PEOPLE

Now all the Cloud People, the Lightning People, the Thunder and Rainbow Peoples followed the Sia into the upper world. But all the people of Tinia, the middle world, did not leave the lower world. Only a portion were sent by the Spider to work for the people of the upper world. The Cloud People are so many that, although the demands of the earth people are so great, there are always many passing about over Tinia for pleasure. These Cloud People ride on wheels, small wheels being used by the little Cloud children and large wheels by the older ones.

The Cloud People keep always behind their masks. The shape of the mask depends upon the number of the people and the work being done. The Henati are the floating white clouds behind which the Cloud People pass for pleasure. The Heash are clouds like the plains and behind these the Cloud People are laboring to water the earth. Water is brought by the Cloud People, from the springs at the base of the mountains, in gourds and jugs and vases by the men, women, and children. They rise from the springs and pass through the trunk of the tree to its top, which reaches Tinia. They pass on to the point to be sprinkled.

The priest of the Cloud People is above even the priests of the Thunder, Lightning, and Rainbow Peoples. The Cloud People have ceremonials, just like those of the Sia. On the altars of the Sia may be seen figures arranged just as the Cloud People sit in their ceremonials.

When a priest of the Cloud People wishes assistance from the Thunder and Lightning Peoples, he notifies their priests, but keeps a supervision of all things himself.

Then the Lightning People shoot their arrows to make it rain the harder. The smaller flashes come from the bows of the children. The Thunder People have human forms, with wings of knives, and by flapping these wings they make a great noise. Thus they frighten the

Cloud and Lightning People into working the harder.

The Rainbow People were created to work in Tinia to make it more beautiful for the people of Ha-arts, the earth, to look upon. The elders make the beautiful rainbows, but the children assist. The Sia have no idea of what or how these bows are made. They do know, however, that war heroes always travel upon the rainbows.

(Sia)

CREATURES

Navajo shaman gives medicine to participant sitting
atop blanket, as two others look on. Circa 1900

WAZIYA, THE WEATHER SPIRIT

The giant called Waziya knows when there is to be a change of weather. He is a giant. When he travels, his footprints are large enough for several Indians to stand in abreast. His strides are very far apart; at one step he can go over a hill.

When it is cold, people say, "Waziya has returned." They used to pray to him, but when they found he paid no attention to him, they ceased to do it.

When warm weather is coming, Waziya wraps himself in a thick robe. But when cold weather is coming, he wears nothing at all. Waziya, the giant god of the north, and Itokaga, the god of the south, are ever battling. Each in turn wins the victory.

(Teton)

WEENDIGOES AND THE BONE-DWARF

In a lonely forest, there once lived a man and his wife, who had a son. The father went forth every day, according to the custom of the Indians, to hunt for food to supply his family.

One day, while he was absent, his wife, on going out of the lodge, looked toward the lake that was near, and she saw a very large man walking on the water, and coming fast toward the lodge. He was already so near that she could not, if she had wished to, escape by flight. She thought to herself, "What shall I say to the monster?"

As he advanced rapidly, she ran in, and taking the hand of her son, a boy of three or four years old, she led him out. Speaking very loud,

"See, my son," she said, "your grandfather;" and then added, in a tone of appeal and supplication, "he will have pity on us."

The giant approached and said, with a loud ha! ha! "Yes, my son;" and added, addressing the woman, "Have you any thing to eat?"

By good luck the lodge was well supplied with meats of various kinds; the woman thought to please him by handing him these, which were savory and carefully prepared. But he pushed them away in disgust, saying, "I smell fire;" and, not waiting to be invited, he seized upon the carcass of a deer which lay by the door, and dispatched it almost without stopping to take breath.

When the hunter came home he was surprised to see the monster, he was so very frightful. He had again brought a deer, which he had no sooner put down than the cannibal seized it, tore it in pieces, and devoured it as though he had been fasting for a week. The hunter looked on in fear and astonishment, and in a whisper he told his wife that he was afraid for their lives, as this monster was one whom Indians call Weendigoes. He did not even dare to speak to him, nor did the cannibal say a word, but as soon as he had finished his meal, he stretched himself down and fell asleep.

In the evening the Weendigo told the people that he should go out a hunting; and he strided away toward the North. Toward morning he returned, all besmeared with blood, but he did not make known where he had been nor of what kind of game he had been in quest; although the hunter and his wife had dreadful suspicions of the sport in which he had been engaged. Withal his hunger did not seem to be staid, for he took up the deer which the hunter had brought in, and devoured it eagerly, leaving the family to make their meal of the dried meats which had been reserved in the lodge.

In this manner the Weendigo and the hunter's family lived for some time, and it surprised them that the monster never attempted their lives; although he never slept at night, but always went out and re-turned, by the break of day, stained with blood, and looking very wild and famished. When there was no deer to be had wherewith to finish his repast, he said nothing. In truth he was always still and gloomy, and he seldom spoke to any of them; when he did, his discourse was chiefly addressed to the boy.

One evening, after he had thus sojourned with them for many weeks, he informed the hunter that the time had now arrived for him to take his leave, but that before doing so, he would give him a charm that would bring good luck to his lodge. He presented to him two arrows, and thanking the hunter and his wife for their kindness, the Weendigo departed, saying, as he left them, that he had all the world to travel over.

The hunter and his wife were happy when he was gone, for they had looked every moment to have been devoured by him. He tried the arrows, and they never failed to bring down whatever they were aimed at.

They had lived on, prosperous and contented, for a year, when, one day, the hunter being absent, his wife on going out of the lodge, saw something like a black cloud approaching.

She looked until it came near, when she perceived that it was another Weendigo or Giant Cannibal. Remembering the good conduct of the other, she had no fear of this one, and asked him to look into the lodge.

He did so; and finding after he had glared around, that there was no food at hand, he grew very wroth, and, being sorely disappointed, he took the lodge and threw it to the winds. He seemed hardly at first to notice the woman in his anger; but presently he cast a fierce glance upon her, and seizing her by the waist, in spite of her cries and entreaties, he bore her off. To the little son, who ran to and fro lamenting, he paid no heed.

At night-fall, when the hunter returned from the forest, he was amazed. His lodge was gone, and he saw his son sitting near the spot where it had stood, shedding tears. The son pointed in the direction the Weendigo had taken, and as the father hurried along he found the remains of his wife strewn upon the ground.

The hunter blackened his face, and vowed in his heart that he would have revenge. He built another lodge, and gathering together the bones of his wife, he placed them in the hollow part of a dry tree.

He left his boy to take care of the lodge while he was absent, hunting and roaming about from place to place, striving to forget his misfortune, and searching for the wicked Weendigo.

He had been gone but a little while one morning, when his son shot his arrows out through the top of the lodge, and running out to look for them, he could find them nowhere. The boy had been trying his luck, and he was puzzled that he had shot his shafts entirely out of sight.

His father made him more arrows, and when he was again left alone, he shot one of them out; but although he looked as sharply as he could toward the spot where it fell, and ran thither at once, he could not find it.

He shot another, which was lost in the same way; and returning to the lodge to replenish his quiver, he happened to espy one of the lucky arrows, which the first Weendigo had given to his father, hanging upon the side of the lodge. He reached up, and having secured it, he shot it out at the opening, and immediately running out to find where it fell, he was surprised to see a beautiful boy just in the act of taking it up, and hurrying away with it to a large tree, where he disappeared.

The hunter's son followed, and having come to the tree, he beheld the face of the boy looking out through an opening in the hollow part.

"Ha! ha!" he said, "my friend, come out and play with me;" and he urged the boy till he consented. They played and shot their arrows by turns.

Suddenly the young boy said, "Your father is coming. We must stop. Promise me that you will not tell him."

The hunter's son promised, and the other disappeared in the tree.

When the hunter returned from the chase, his son sat demurely by the fire. In the course of the evening he asked his father to make him a new bow; and when he was questioned as to the use he could find for two bows, he answered that one might break or get lost.

The father pleased at his son's diligence in the practice of the bow, made him the two weapons; and the next day, as soon as his father had gone away, the boy ran to the hollow tree, and invited his little friend to come out and play; at the same time presenting to him the new bow. They went and played in the lodge together, and in their sport they raised the ashes all over it.

Suddenly again the youngest said, "Your father is coming, I must leave."

He again exacted a promise of secresy, and went back to his tree. The eldest took his seat near the fire.

When the hunter came in he was surprised to see the ashes scattered about. "Why, my son," he said, "you must have played very hard to day to raise such a dust all alone."

"Yes," the boy answered, "I was very lonesome, and I ran round and round—that is the cause of it."

The next day the hunter made ready for the chase as usual. The boy said, "Father, try and hunt all day, and see what you can kill."

He had no sooner set out than the boy called his friend, and they played and chased each other round the lodge. They had great delight in each other's company, and made merry by the hour. The hunter was again returning, and came to a rising ground, which caught the winds as they passed, and he heard his son laughing and making a noise, but the sounds as they reached him on the hill-top, seemed as if they arose from two persons playing.

At the same time the younger boy stopped, and after saying "Your father is coming," he stole away, under cover of the high grass, to his hollow tree, which was not far off.

The hunter, on entering, found his son sitting by the fire, very quiet and unconcerned, although he saw that all the articles of the lodge were lying thrown about in all directions.

"Why, my son," he said "you must play very hard every day; and what is it that you do, all alone, to throw the lodge in such confusion?"

The boy again had his excuse. "Father," he answered, "I play in this manner: I chase and drag my blanket around the lodge, and that is the reason you see the ashes spread about."

The hunter was not satisfied until his son had shown him how he played with the blanket, which he did so adroitly as to set his father laughing, and at last drive him out of the lodge with the great clouds of ashes that he raised.

The next morning the boy renewed his request that his father should be absent all day, and see if he could not kill two deer. The hunter thought this a strange desire on the part of his son, but as he had always humored the boy, he went into the forest as usual, bent on accomplishing his wish, if he could.

As soon as he was out of sight, his son hastened to his young companion at the tree, and they continued their sports.

The father on nearing his home in the evening, as he reached the rising ground, again heard the sounds of play and laughter; and as the wind brought them straight to his ear, he was now certain that there were two voices.

The boy from the tree had no more than time to escape, when the hunter entered, and found his son, sitting as usual, near the fire. When he cast his eyes around, he saw that the lodge was in greater confusion than before. "My son," he said, "you must be very foolish when alone to play so. But, tell me, my son; I heard two voices, I am sure;" and he looked closely on the prints of the footsteps in the ashes. "True," he continued, "here is the print of a foot which is smaller than my son's;" and he was now satisfied that his suspicions were well founded, and that some very young person had been the companion of his son.

The boy could not now refuse to tell his father what had happened.

"Father," he said, "I found a boy in the hollow of that tree, near the lodge, where you placed my mother's bones."

Strange thoughts came over the mind of the hunter; did his wife live again in this beautiful child?

Fearful of disturbing the dead, he did not dare to visit the place where he had deposited her remains.

He, however, engaged his son to entice the boy to a dead tree, by the edge of a wood, where they could kill many flying-squirrels by setting it on fire. He said that he would conceal himself near by, and take the boy.

The next day the hunter accordingly went into the woods, and his son, calling the boy from the tree, urged him to go with him to kill the squirrels. The boy objected that his father was near, but he was at length prevailed on to go, and after they had fired the tree, and while they were busy killing or taking the squirrels, the hunter suddenly made his appearance, and clasped the strange boy in his arms. He cried out, "Kago, kago, don't, don't. You will tear my clothes!" for he was clad in a fine apparel, which shone as if it had been made of a beautiful transparent skin. The father reassured him by every means in his power.

By constant kindness and gentle words the boy was reconciled to remain with them; but chiefly by the presence of his young friend, the hunter's son, to whom he was fondly attached. The children were never parted from each other; and when the hunter looked upon the strange boy, he seemed to see living in him the better spirit of his lost wife. He was thankful to the Great Spirit for this act of goodness, and in his heart he felt assured that in time the boy would show great virtue, and in some way avenge him on the wicked Weendigo who had destroyed the companion of his lodge.

The hunter grew at ease in his spirit, and gave all of the time he could spare from the chase to the society of the two children; but, what affected him the most, both of his sons, although they were well-formed and beautiful, grew no more in stature, but remained children still. Every day they resembled each other more and more, and they never ceased to sport and divert themselves in the innocent ways of childhood.

One day the hunter had gone abroad with his bow and arrows, leaving, at the request of the strange boy, one of the two shafts which the friendly Weendigo had given to him, behind in the lodge.

When he returned, what were his surprise and joy to see stretched dead by his lodge-door, the black giant who had slain his wife. He had been stricken down by the magic shaft in the hands of the little stranger from the tree; and ever after the boy, or the Bone-Dwarf as he was called, was the guardian and good genius of the lodge, and no evil spirit, giant, or Weendigo, dared approach it to mar their peace.

BOG MYTH

Bogs are very mysterious. Strange things, with thick hair, remain at the bottom of a bog. These things have no eyes, but they eat everything which comes to them, and from their bodies water flows always. When one of these Beings wishes, he changes his place of abode. He lives at a new place. Then the old place where he lived dries up; but a fresh spring of water gushes from his new lodge. The water of this spring is warm in winter; but in summer it is as cold as ice. Before one dares drink of it, he prays to the water, else he may bring illness on himself for irreverence.

In the olden days, one of the Bog Beings was pulled out of a bog and carried to the camp. A special tepee was built for him. But so much water flowed all around that the people were almost drowned. Then those who were not drowned offered him food. He sat motionless, gazing at them. But the food vanished before they could see it go; and no one saw the Bog Being eat it.

(Dakota)

THE THUNDER BIRD

In the olden times, a hunter once shot at a large bird which was flying above him. It fell to the ground. It was so large he was afraid to go to it alone, so he went back to the camp for others.

When they came back to the place where the bird had been shot, thunder was rolling through the ravine. Flashes of lightning showed the place where the bird lay. They came nearer. Then the lightning flashed so that they could not see the bird. One flash killed a hunter.

The other Indians fled back to the camp. They knew it was the Thunder Bird.

Once the Thunder Bird, in the days of the grandfathers, came down to the ground and alighted there. You may know that is so, because the grass remains burned off a large space, and the outlines are those of a large bird with outspread wings.

(Comanche)

THE MAN-FISH

A very great while ago the ancestors of the Shawanos nation lived on the other side of the Great Lake, half-way between the rising sun and the evening star. It was a land of deep snows and much frost, of winds which whistled in the clear, cold nights, and storms which travelled from seas no eyes could reach. Sometimes the sun ceased to shine for moons together, and then he was continually before their eyes for as many more. In the season of cold the waters were all locked up, and the snows overtopped the ridge of the cabins. Then he shone out so fiercely that men fell stricken by his fierce rays, and were numbered with the snow that had melted and run to the embrace of the rivers. It was not like the beautiful lands—the lands blessed with soft suns and ever-green vales—in which the Shawanos now dwell, yet it was well stocked with deer, and the waters with fat seals and great fish, which were caught just when the people pleased to go after them. Still, the nation were discontented, and wished to leave their barren and inhospitable shores. The priests had told them of a beautiful world beyond the Great Salt Lake, from which the glorious sun never disappeared for a longer time than the duration of a child's sleep, where snow-shoes were never wanted—a land clothed with perpetual verdure, and bright with never-failing gladness. The Shawanos listened to these tales till they came to loathe their own simple comforts; all they talked of, all they appeared to think of, was the land of the happy hunting-grounds.

Once upon a time the people were much terrified at seeing a strange creature, much resembling a man, riding along the waves of the lake on the borders of which they dwelt. He had on his head long green hair; his face was shaped like that of a porpoise, and he had a beard of the colour of ooze.

If the people were frightened at seeing a man who could live in the water like a fish or a duck, how much more were they frightened when they saw that from his breast down he was actually fish, or rather two fishes, for each of his legs was a whole and distinct fish. When they heard him speak distinctly in their own language, and when he sang songs sweeter than the music of birds in spring, or the whispers of love from the lips of a beautiful maiden, they thought it a being from the Land of Shades—a spirit from the happy fishing-grounds beyond the lake of storms.

He would sit for a long time, his fish-legs coiled up under him, singing to the wondering ears of the Indians upon the shore the pleasures he experienced, and the beautiful and strange things he saw in the depths of the ocean, always closing his strange stories with these words, shouted at the top of his voice—

"Follow me, and see what I will show you."

Every day, when the waves were still and the winds had gone to their resting-place in the depths of the earth, the monster was sure to be seen near the shore where the Shawanos dwelt. For a great many suns they dared not venture upon the water in quest of food, doing nothing but wander along the beach, watching the strange creature as he played his antics upon the surface of the waves, listening to his songs and to his invitation—

"Follow me, and see what I will show you."

The longer he stayed the less they feared him. They became used to him, and in time looked upon him as a spirit who was not made for harm, nor wished to injure the poor Indian. Then they grew hungry, and their wives and little ones cried for food, and, as hunger banishes all fear, in a few days three canoes with many men and warriors ventured off to the rocks in quest of fish.

When they reached the fishing-place, they heard as before the voice shouting—

"Follow me, and see what I will show you."

Presently the man-fish appeared, sitting on the water, with his legs folded under him, and his arms crossed on his breast, as they had usually seen him. There he sat, eying them attentively. When they failed to draw in the fish they had hooked, he would make the water shake and the deep echo with shouts of laughter, and would clap his hands with great noise, and cry—

"Ha, ha! there he fooled you."

When a fish was caught he was very angry. When the fishers had tried long and patiently, and taken little, and the sun was just hiding itself behind the dark clouds which skirted the region of warm winds, the strange creature cried out still stronger than before—

"Follow me, and see what I will show you."

Kiskapocoke, who was the head man of the tribe, asked him what he wanted, but he would make no other answer than—

"Follow me."

"Do you think," said Kiskapocoke, "I would be such a fool as to go I don't know with whom, and I don't know where?"

"See what I will show you," cried the man-fish.

"Can you show us anything better than we have yonder?" asked the warrior.

"I will show you," replied the monster, "a land where there is a herd of deer for every one that skips over your hills, where there are vast droves of creatures larger than your sea-elephants, where there is no cold to freeze you, where the sun is always soft and smiling, where the trees are always in bloom."

The people began to be terrified, and wished themselves on land, but the moment they tried to paddle towards the shore, some invisible hand would seize their canoes and draw them back, so that an hour's labour did not enable them to gain the length of their boat in the direction of their homes. At last Kiskapocoke said to his companions—

"What shall we do?"

"Follow me," said the fish.

Then Kiskapocoke said to his companions—

"Let us follow him, and see what will come of it."

So they followed him,—he swimming and they paddling, until night came. Then a great wind and deep darkness prevailed, and the Great Serpent commenced hissing in the depths of the ocean. The people were terribly frightened, and did not think to live till another sun, but the man-fish kept close to the boats, and bade them not be afraid, for nothing should hurt them.

When morning came, nothing could be seen of the shore they had left. The winds still raged, the seas were very high, and the waters ran into their canoes like melted snows over the brows of the mountains, but the man-fish handed them large shells, with which they baled the water out. As they had brought neither food nor water with them, they had become both hungry and thirsty. Kiskapocoke told the strange creature they wanted to eat and drink, and that he must supply them with what they required.

"Very well," said the man-fish, and, disappearing in the depths of the water, he soon reappeared, bringing with him a bag of parched corn and a shell full of sweet water.

For two moons and a half the fishermen followed the man-fish, till at last one morning their guide exclaimed—

"Look there!"

Upon that they looked in the direction he pointed out to them and saw land, high land, covered with great trees, and glittering as the sand of the Spirit's Island. Behind the shore rose tall mountains, from the tops of which issued great flames, which shot up into the sky, as the forks of the lightning cleave the clouds in the hot moon. The waters of the Great Salt Lake broke in small waves upon its shores, which were covered with sporting seals and wild ducks pluming themselves in the beams of the warm and gentle sun. Upon the shore stood a great many strange people, but when they saw the strangers step upon the land and the man-fish, they fled to the woods like startled deer, and were no more seen.

When the warriors were safely landed, the man-fish told them to let the canoe go; "for," said he, "you will never need it more." They had travelled but a little way into the woods when he bade them stay where they were, while he told the spirit of the land that the strangers he had promised were come, and with that he descended into a deep cave near at hand. He soon returned, accompanied by a creature as strange in appearance as himself. His legs and feet were those of a man. He had leggings and moccasins like an Indian's, tightly laced and beautifully decorated with wampum, but his head was like a goat's. He talked like a man, and his language was one well understood by the strangers.

"I will lead you," he said, "to a beautiful land, to a most beautiful land, men from the clime of snows. There you will find all the joys an Indian covets."

For many moons the Shawanos travelled under the guidance of the man-goat, into whose hands the man-fish had put them, when he retraced his steps to the Great Lake. They came at length to the land which the Shawanos now occupy. They found it as the strange spirits had described it. They married the daughters of the land, and their numbers increased till they were so many that no one could count them. They grew strong, swift, and valiant in war, keen and patient in the chase. They overcame all the tribes eastward of the River of Rivers, and south to the shore of the Great Lake.

PUCK WUDJ ININEES

There was a time when all the inhabitants of the earth had died, excepting two helpless children, a baby boy and a little girl. When their parents died, these children were asleep. The little girl, who was the elder, was the first to wake. She looked around her, but seeing nobody besides her little brother, who lay asleep, she quietly resumed her bed. At the end of ten days her brother moved without opening his eyes. At the end of ten days more he changed his position, lying on the other side.

The girl soon grew up to woman's estate, but the boy increased in stature very slowly. It was a long time before he could even creep. When he was able to walk, his sister made him a little bow and arrows, and suspended around his neck a small shell, saying, you shall be called Wa-Dais-Ais-Imid, or He of the Little Shell. Every day he would go out with his little bow, shooting at the small birds. The first bird he killed was a tomtit. His sister was highly pleased when he took it to her. She carefully skinned and stuffed it, and put it away for him. The next day he killed a red squirrel. His sister preserved this too. The third day he killed a partridge (Peéna), which she stuffed and set up. After this, he acquired more courage, and would venture some distance from home. His skill and success as a hunter daily increased, and he killed the deer, bear, moose, and other large animals inhabiting the forest. In fine he became a great hunter.

He had now arrived to maturity of years, but remained a perfect infant in stature. One day, walking about, he came to a small lake. It was in the winter season. He saw a man on the ice killing beavers. He appeared to be a giant. Comparing himself to this great man he appeared no bigger than an insect. He seated himself on the shore, and watched his movements. When the large man had killed many beavers, he put them on a hand sled which he had, and pursued his way home. When he saw him retire, he followed him, and wielding his magic shell, cut off the tail of one of the beavers, and ran home with his trophy. When the tall stranger reached his lodge, with his sled load of beavers, he was surprised to find the tail of one of them gone, for he had not observed the movements of the little hero of the shell.

The next day Wa-Dis-Ais-Imid, went to the same lake. The man had already fixed his load of beavers on his odaw'bon, or sled, and commenced his return. But he nimbly ran forward, and overtaking him, succeeded, by the same means, in securing another of the beaver's tails. When the man saw that he had lost another of this most esteemed part of the animal, he was very angry. I wonder, said he, what dog it is, that has thus cheated me. Could I meet him, I would make his flesh quiver at the point of my lance. Next day he pursued his hunting at the beaver dam near the lake, and was followed again by the little man of the shell. On this occasion the hunter had used so much expedition, that he had accomplished his object, and nearly reached his home, before our tiny hero could overtake him. He nimbly drew his shell and cut off another beaver's tail. In all these pranks, he availed himself of his power of invisibility, and thus escaped observation. When the man saw that the trick had been so often repeated, his anger was greater than ever. He gave vent to his feelings in words. He looked carefully around to see whether he could discover any tracks. But he could find none. His unknown visitor had stepped so lightly as to leave no track.

Next day he resolved to disappoint him by going to his beaver pond very early. When Wa-Dais-Ais-Imid reached the place, he found the fresh traces of his work, but he had already returned. He followed his tracks, but failed to overtake him. When he came in sight of the lodge the stranger was in front of it, employed in skinning his beavers. As he stood looking at him, he thought, I will let him see me. Presently the man, who proved to be no less a personage than Manabozho, looked up and saw him. After regarding him with attention, "Who are you, little man," said Manabozho. "I have a mind to kill you." The little hero of the shell replied, "If you were to try to kill me you could not do it."

When he returned home he told his sister that they must separate. "I must go away," said he, "it is my fate. You too," he added, "must go away soon. Tell me where you would wish to dwell." She said, "I would like to go to the place of the breaking of daylight. I have always loved the east. The earliest glimpses of light are from that quarter, and it is, to my mind, the most beautiful part of the heavens. After I get there, my brother, whenever you see the clouds in that direction of various colors, you may think that your sister is painting her face."

"And I," said he, "my sister, shall live on the mountains and rocks. There I can see you at the earliest hour, and there the streams of water are clear, and the air pure. And I shall ever be called Puck Wudj Ininee, or the little wild man of the mountains."

"But," he resumed, "before we part forever, I must go and try to find some Manitoes." He left her, and travelled over the surface of the globe, and then went far down into the earth. He had been treated well wherever he went. At last he found a giant Manito, who had a large kettle which was forever boiling. The giant regarded him with a stern look, and then took him up in his hand, and threw him unceremoniously into the kettle. But by the protection of his personal spirit, he was shielded from harm, and with much ado got out of it and escaped. He returned to his sister, and related his rovings and misadventures. He finished his story by addressing her thus: "My sister, there is a Manito, at each of the four corners of the earth. There is also one above them, far in the sky; and last," continued he, "there is another, and wicked one, who lives deep down in the earth. We must now separate. When the winds blow from the four corners of the earth you must then go. They will carry you to the place you wish. I go to the rocks and mountains, where my kindred will ever delight to dwell." He then took his ball stick, and commenced running up a high mountain, whooping as he went. Presently the winds blew, and, as he predicted, his sister was borne by them to the eastern sky, where she has ever since been, and her name is the Morning Star.

Blow, winds, blow! my sister lingers
For her dwelling in the sky,
Where the morn, with rosy fingers,
Shall her cheeks with vermil dye.

There, my earliest views directed,
Shall from her their color take,
And her smiles, through clouds reflected,
Guide me on, by wood or lake.

While I range the highest mountains,

Sport in valleys green and low,
Or beside our Indian fountains
Raise my tiny hip holla.

(Ojibwa)

THE WOLF BROTHER

A solitary lodge stood on the banks of a remote lake. It was near the hour of sunset. Silence reigned within and without. Not a sound was heard but the low breathing of the dying inmate and head of this poor family. His wife and three children surrounded his bed. Two of the latter were almost grown up: the other was a mere child. All their simple skill in medicine had been exhausted to no effect. They moved about the lodge in whispers, and were waiting the departure of the spirit. As one of the last acts of kindness, the skin door of the lodge had been thrown back to admit the fresh air. The poor man felt a momentary return of strength, and, raising himself a little, addressed his family.

"I leave you in a world of care, in which it has required all my strength and skill to supply you food, and protect you from the storms and cold of a severe climate. For you, my partner in life, I have less sorrow in parting, because I am persuaded you will not remain long behind me, and will therefore find the period of your sufferings shortened. But you, my children! my poor and forsaken children, who have just commenced the career of life, who will protect you from its evils? Listen to my words! Unkindness, ingratitude, and every wickedness is in the scene before you. It is for this cause that, years ago, I withdrew from my kindred and my tribe, to spend my days in this lonely spot. I have contented myself with the company of your mother and yourselves during seasons of very frequent scarcity and want, while your kindred, feasting in a scene where food is plenty, have caused the forests to echo with the shouts of successful war. I gave up these things for the enjoyment of peace. I wished to shield you from the bad examples you would inevitably have followed. I have seen you, thus far, grow up in innocence. If we have sometimes suffered bodily want, we have escaped pain of mind.[61] We have been kept from scenes of rioting and bloodshed.

"My career is now at its close. I will shut my eyes in peace, if you, my children, will promise me to cherish each other. Let not your mother suffer during the few days that are left to her; and I charge you, on no account, to forsake your youngest brother. Of him I give you both my dying charge to take a tender care." He sank exhausted on his pallet. The family waited a moment, as if expecting to hear something further; but, when they came to his side, the spirit had taken its flight.

The mother and daughter gave vent to their feelings in lamentations. The elder son witnessed the scene in silence. He soon exerted himself to supply, with the bow and net, his father's place. Time, however, wore away heavily. Five moons had filled and waned, and the sixth was near its full, when the mother also died. In her last moments she pressed the fulfilment of their promise to their father, which the children readily renewed, because they were yet free from selfish motives.

The winter passed; and the spring, with its enlivening effects in a northern hemisphere, cheered the drooping spirits of the bereft little family. The girl, being the eldest, dictated to her brothers, and seemed to feel a tender and sisterly affection for the youngest, who was rather sickly and delicate. The other boy soon showed symptoms of restlessness and ambition, and addressed the sister as follows: "My sister, are we always to live as if there were no other human beings in the world? Must I deprive myself of the pleasure of associating with my own kind? I have determined this question for myself. I shall seek the villages of men, and you cannot prevent me."

The sister replied: "I do not say no, my brother, to what you desire. We are not prohibited the society of our fellow-mortals; but we are told to cherish each other, and to do nothing independent of each other. Neither pleasure nor pain ought, therefore, to separate us, especially from our younger brother, who being but a child, and weakly withal, is entitled to a double share of our affection. If we follow our separate gratifications, it will surely make us neglect him, whom we are bound by vows, both to our father and mother, to support." The young man received this address in silence. He appeared daily to grow more restive and moody, and one day, taking his bow and arrows, left the lodge and never returned.

Affection nerved the sister's arm. She was not so ignorant of the forest arts as to let her brother want. For a long time she administered to his necessities, and supplied a mother's cares. At length, however, she began to be weary of solitude and of her charge. No one came to be a witness of her assiduity, or to let fall a single word in her native language. Years, which added to her strength and capability of directing the affairs of the household, brought with them the irrepressible desire of society, and made solitude irksome. At this point, selfishness gained the ascendency of her heart; for, in meditating a change in her mode of life, she lost sight of her younger brother, and left him to be provided for by contingencies.

One day, after collecting all the provisions she had been able to save for emergencies, after bringing a quantity of wood to the door, she said to her little brother: "My brother, you must not stray from the lodge. I am going to seek our elder brother. I shall be back soon." Then, taking her bundle, she set off in search of habitations. She soon found them, and was so much taken up with the pleasures and amusements of social life, that the thought of her brother was almost entirely obliterated. She accepted proposals of marriage; and, after that, thought still less of her hapless and abandoned relative.

Meantime her elder brother had also married, and lived on the shores of the same lake whose ample circuit contained the abandoned lodge of his father and his forsaken brother. The latter was soon brought to the pinching turn of his fate. As soon as he had eaten all the food left by his sister, he was obliged to pick berries and dig up roots. These were finally covered by the snow. Winter came on with all its rigors. He was obliged to quit the lodge in search of other food. Sometimes he passed the night in the clefts of old trees or caverns, and ate the refuse meals of the wolves. The latter, at last, became his only resource; and he became so fearless of these animals that he would sit close by them while they devoured their prey. The wolves, on the other hand, became so familiar with his face and form, that they were undisturbed by his approach; and, appearing to sympathize with him in his outcast condition, would always leave something for his repast. In this way he lived till spring. As soon as the lake was free from ice, he followed his new-found friends themselves to the shore. It happened, the same day, that his elder brother was fishing in his canoe, a considerable distance out in the lake, when he thought he heard the cries of a child on the shore, and wondered how any could exist on so bleak and barren a part of the coast. He listened again attentively, and distinctly heard the cry repeated. He made for shore as quick as possible, and, as he approached land, discovered and recognized his little brother, and heard him singing, in a plaintive voice—

Neesia—neesia,
Shyegwuh goosuh!
Ni my een gwun iewh!
Ni my een gwun iewh!
Heo hwooh.
My brother—my brother,
Ah! see, I am turning into a wolf.

At the termination of his song, which was drawn out with a peculiar cadence, he howled like a wolf. The elder brother was still more astonished, when, getting nearer shore, he perceived his poor brother partly transformed into that animal. He immediately leaped on shore, and strove to catch him in his arms, soothingly saying, "My brother, my brother, come to me." But the boy eluded his grasp, crying as he fled, "Neesia, neesia," and howling in the intervals.

The elder brother, conscience stricken, and feeling his brotherly affection strongly return, with redoubled force exclaimed, in great anguish, "My brother! my brother! my brother!"

But, the nearer he approached, the more rapidly the transformation went on; the boy alternately singing and howling, and calling out the name, first of his brother, and then of his sister, till the change was completely accomplished, when he exclaimed, "I am a wolf!" and bounded out of sight.

(Ojibwa)

THE WOMAN AND THE WATER TIGER

There was an old hag of a woman living with her daughter-in-law, and son, and a little orphan boy, whom she was bringing up. When her son-in-law came home from hunting, it was his custom to bring his wife the moose's lip, the kidney of the bear, or some other choice bits of different animals. These she would cook crisp, so as to make a sound with her teeth in eating them. This kind attention of the hunter to his wife at last excited the envy of the old woman. She wished to have the same luxuries, and in order to get them she finally resolved to make way with her son's wife. One day, she asked her to leave her infant son to the care of the orphan boy, and come out and swing with her. She took her to the shore of a lake, where there was a high range of rocks overhanging the water. Upon the top of this rock, she erected a swing. She then undressed, and fastened a piece of leather around her body, and commenced swinging, going over the precipice at every swing. She continued it but a short time, when she told her daughter to do the same. The daughter obeyed. She undressed, and tying the leather string as she was directed, began swinging. When the swing had got in full motion and well a-going, so that it went clear beyond the precipice at every sweep, the old woman slyly cut the cords and let her daughter drop into the lake. She then put on her daughter's clothing, and thus disguised went home in the dusk of the evening and counterfeited her appearance and duties. She found the child crying, and gave it the breast, but it would not draw. The orphan boy asked her where its mother was. She answered, "She is still swinging." He said, "I shall go and look for her." "No!" said she, "you must not—what should you go for?" When the husband came in, in the evening, he gave the coveted morsel to his supposed wife. He missed his mother-in-law, but said nothing. She eagerly ate the dainty, and tried to keep the child still. The husband looked rather astonished to see his wife studiously averting her face, and asked her why the child cried so. She said, she did not know—that it would not draw.

In the mean time, the orphan boy went to the lake shores, and found no one. He mentioned his suspicions, and while the old woman was out getting wood, he told him all he had heard or seen. The man then painted his face black, and placed his spear upside down in the earth, and requested the Great Spirit to send lightning, thunder, and rain, in the hope that the body of his wife might arise from the water. He then began to fast, and told the boy to take the child and play on the lake shore.

We must now go back to the swing. After the wife had plunged into the lake, she found herself taken hold of by a water-tiger, whose tail twisted itself round her body, and drew her to the bottom. There she found a fine lodge, and all things ready for her reception, and she became the wife of the water-tiger. Whilst the children were playing along the shore, and the boy was casting pebbles into the lake, he saw a gull coming from its centre, and flying towards the shore, and when on shore, the bird immediately assumed the human shape. When he looked again, he recognized the lost mother. She had a leather belt around her loins, and another belt of white metal, which was, in reality, the tail of the water-tiger, her husband. She suckled the babe, and said to the boy—"Come here with him, whenever he cries, and I will nurse him."

The boy carried the child home, and told these things to the father. When the child again cried, the father went also with the boy to the lake shore, and hid himself in a clump of trees. Soon the appearance of a gull was seen, with a long shining belt, or chain, and as soon as it came to the shore, it assumed the mother's shape, and she began to suckle the child. The husband had brought along his spear, and seeing the shining chain, he boldly struck it and broke the links apart. He then took his wife and child home, with the orphan boy. When they entered the lodge, the old woman looked up, but it was a look of despair; she instantly dropped her head. A rustling was heard in the lodge, and the next moment she leaped up and flew out of the lodge, and was never heard of more.

(Odjibwa)

THE GIRL-CHENOO

Of the old time. Far up the Saguenay River a branch turns off to the north, running back into the land of ice and snow. Ten families went up this stream one autumn in their canoes, to be gone all winter on a hunt. Among them was a beautiful girl, twenty years of age. A young man in the band wished her to become his wife, but she flatly refused him. Perhaps she did it in such a way as to wound his pride; certainly she roused all that was savage in him, and he gave up all his mind to revenge. He was skilled in medicine, or in magic, so he went into the woods and gathered an herb which makes people insensible. Then stealing into the lodge when all were asleep, he held it to the girl's face, until she had inhaled the odor and could not be easily awakened. Going out he made a ball of snow, and returning placed it in the hollow of her neck, in front, just below the throat. Then he retired without being discovered. So she could not awake, while the chill went to her heart.

When she awoke she was chilly, shivering, and sick. She refused to eat. This lasted long, and her parents became alarmed. They inquired what ailed her. She was ill-tempered; she said that nothing was the matter. One day, having been sent to the spring for water, she remained absent so long that her mother went to seek her. Approaching unseen, she observed her greedily eating snow. And asking her what it meant, the daughter explained that she felt within a burning sensation, which the snow relieved. More than that, she craved the snow; the taste of it was pleasant to her.

After a few days she began to grow fierce, as though she wished to kill some one. At last she begged her parents to kill her. Hitherto she had loved them very much. Now she told them that unless they killed her she would certainly be their death. Her whole nature was being changed.

"How can we kill you?" her mother asked.

"You must shoot at me," she replied, "with seven arrows. And if you can kill me with seven shots, all will be well. But if you cannot, I shall kill you."

Seven men shot at her, as she sat in the wigwam. She was not bound.

Every arrow struck her in the breast, but she sat firm and unmoved.

Forty-nine times they pierced her; from time to time she looked up with an encouraging smile. When the last arrow struck she fell dead.

Then they burned the body, as she had directed. It was soon reduced to ashes, with the exception of the heart, which was of the hardest ice. This required much time to melt and break. At last all was over.

She had been brought under the power of an evil spirit; she was rapidly being changed into a Chenoo a wild, fierce, unconquerable being. But she knew it all the while, and it was against her will. So she begged that she might be killed.

The Indians left the place; since that day none have ever returned to it. They feared lest some small part of the body might have remained unconsumed, and that from it another Chenoo would rise, capable of killing all whom she met.

(Micmac.)

GIANT MAGICIANS

There was once a man and his wife who lived by the sea, far away from other people. They had many children, and they were very poor. One day this couple were in their canoe, far from land. There came up a dense fog; they were quite lost.

They heard a noise as of paddles and voices. It drew nearer. They saw dimly a monstrous canoe filled with giants, who greeted the little folk like friends. "Uch keen, tahmee wejeaok?" "My little brother," said the leader, "where are you going?" "I am lost in the fog," said the poor Indian, very sadly. "Ah, come with us to our camp," said the giant, who seemed to be a good fellow, if there ever was one. "Truly, ye will be well treated, my small friends, for my father is the chief; so be of good cheer!" And they, being much amazed at this gentleness, sat still in awe, while two of the giants, each putting a tip of his paddle under their bark, lifted it up and put it into their own, as if it had been a chip. And truly the giants seemed to be as much pleased with the little folk as a boy would be who had found a flying squirrel.

And as they drew near the beach, lo! they beheld three wigwams, high as mountains, in size according to that of the giants. And coming to meet them was the chief, who was taller than the rest.

"Ha!" he cried. "Son, what have you there? Where did you pick up that little brother?" "Noo, my father, I found him lost in the fog." "Well, bring him home to the lodge, my son!" So the giant took the small canoe in the palm of his hand, the man and his wife sitting therein, and carried them home. Then they were taken into the wigwam, and the canoe was laid carefully in the eaves, but within easy reach, about a hundred and fifty yards from the ground.

Then an abundant meal was set before them, but the benevolent host, mindful of their small size, did not give them more to eat than they would have needed for about ten years to come, and informed them in a subdued whisper, which could hardly have been heard a hundred miles off, that his name was Oscoon.

Now it came to pass, a few days after, that a company of these well-grown people went hunting, and when they returned the guests must needs pity them that they had no game in their land which answered to their size; for they came in with strings of such small affairs as two or three dozen caribou hanging in their belts, as a Micmac would carry a string of squirrels, and swinging one or two moose in their hands like rabbits. Yet, what with these and many deer, bears, and beavers, they made up in the weight of their game what it lacked in size, and of what they had they were generous.

Now the giants became very fond of the small folk, and would not for the world that they should in any way come to harm. And it came to pass that one morning the chief told them that they were to have a grand battle, since they expected in three days to be attacked by a Chenoo. Therefore the Micmac saw that in all things it was even with the giants as with his own people at home, they having their troubles with the wicked, and the chiefs their share in being obliged to keep up their magic and know all that was going on in the world. Yea, for he would be a poor powwow and a necromancer worth nothing who could not foretell such a trifle as the day and hour when an enemy would be on them!

But this time the sagamore, was forewarned, and bade his little guests stop their ears and bind up their heads, and roll themselves in many folds of dressed skins, lest they should hear the deadly war-scream of the Chenoo. And with all their care they hardly survived it; but the second scream hurt them less; and after the third the chief came to them with a cheerful countenance, and bade them arise and unpack themselves, for the monster was slain, and though his four sons, with two other giants, had been sorely tried, yet they had conquered.

But the sorrows of the good are never at an end, and so it was with these honest giants, who were always being pestered with some kind of scurvy knaves or others who would not leave them in peace. For anon the chief announced that this time a Kookwes—a burly, beastly villain, not two points better than his cousin the Chenoo—was coming to play at rough murder with them. And, verily, by this time the Micmac began to believe, without bating an ace on it, that all of these tall people were like the wolves, who, meeting with nobody else, bite one another. So they were bound and bundled up as before, and put to bed like dolls. And again they heard the horrible shout, the moderate shout, and the smaller shout, until sooel moonoodooahdigool, which, being interpreted, meaneth that they hardly heard him at all.

Then the warriors, returning, gave proof that they had indeed done something more than kick the wind, for they were covered with blood, and their legs were stuck full of large pines, with here and there an oak or hemlock, for the fight had been in a forest; so that they had been as much troubled as men would be with thistles, nettles, and pine splinters, which is truly often a great trouble. But this was their least trial, for, as they told their chief, the enemy had well-nigh made Jack Drum's entertainment for them, and led them the devil's dance, had not one of them, by good luck, opened his eye for him with a rock which drove it into his brain. And as it was, the chiefs youngest son had been so mauled that, coming home, he fell dead just before his father's door. Truly this might have been deemed almost an accident in some families; but lo! what a good thing it is to have an enchanter in the house, especially one who knows his business, as did the old chief, who, going out, asked the young man why he was lying there. To which he replying that it was because he was dead, his father bade him rise and walk, which he did straight to the supper table, and ate none the less for it.

Now the old chief, thinking that perhaps, his dear little people found life dull and devoid of incident with him, asked them if they were aweary of him. They, with golden truth indeed, answered that they had never been so merry, but that they were anxious as to their children at home. He answered that they were indeed right, and that the next morning they might depart. So their canoe was reached down for them, and packed full of the finest furs and best meat, when they were told to tebah'-dikw', or get in. Then a small dog was put in, and this dog was solemnly charged that he should take the people home, while the people were told to paddle in the direction in which the dog should point. And to the Micmac he said, "Seven years hence you will be reminded of me." And then tokooboosijik (off they went). The man sat in the stern, his wife in the prow, and the dog in the middle of the canoe. The dog pointed, the Indian paddled, the water was smooth. They soon reached home; the children with joy ran to meet them; the dog as joyfully ran to see the children, wagging his tail with great glee, just as if he had been like any other dog, and not a fairy. For, having made acquaintance, he without delay turned tail and trotted off for home again, running over the ocean surface as if it had been hard ice; which might, indeed, have once astonished the good man and his wife, but they had of late days seen so many wonders that they were past marveling.

Now this Indian, who had in the past been always poor, seemed to have quite recovered from that complaint. When he let down his lines the biggest fish bit; all his sprats were salmon; he prayed for goslings, and got geese; moose were as mice to him now; yea, he had the best in the land, with all the fatness thereof. So seven years passed away, and then, as he slept, there came unto him divers dreams, and in them he went back to the Land of the Giants, and saw all those who had been so kind to him. And yet again he dreamed one night that he was standing by his wigwam near the sea, and that a great whale swam up to him and began to sing, and that the singing was the sweetest he had ever heard.

Then he remembered that the giant had told him he would think of him in seven years; and it came clearly before him what it all meant, and that he was erelong to have magical power given to him, and that he should become a Megumoowessoo. This he told his wife, who, not being learned in darksome lore, would fain know more nearly what kind of a being he expected to be, and whether a spirit or a man, good or bad; which was, indeed, not easy to explain, nor is it clearly set down in the chronicles beyond this,—that, whatever it might be, it was all for the best, and that there was a great deal of magic in it.

That day they saw a great shark cruising about in their bay, chasing fish, and this they held for an evil omen. But, soon after, there came trotting towards them over the sea the same small dog who had been their pilot from the Land of the Giants. So he, full of joy, as before, at seeing them and the children, wagged his tail and danced for glee, and then looked earnestly at the man as if for some message. And to him the man said, "It is well. In three years' time I will make you a visit. I will look to the southwest." Then the dog licked the hands and the ears and the eyes of the man, and went home as before over the sea, running on the water.

And when the three years had passed the Indian entered his canoe, and, paddling without fear, found his way to the Land of the Giants. He saw the wigwams standing on the beach; the immense canoes were drawn up on the water's edge; from afar he beheld the old giant coming down to welcome him. But he was alone. And when he had been welcomed, and was in the wigwam, he learned that all the sons were dead. They had died three years before, when the shark, the great sorcerer, had been seen.

They had gone, and the old man had but lingered a little longer. They had made the magic change, they had departed, and he would soon join them in his own kingdom. But ere he went he would leave their great inheritance, their magic, to the man.

Therewith the giant brought out his son's clothes, and bade the Indian put them on. Truly this was as if he had been asked to clothe himself with a great house, since the smallest fold in them would have been to him as a cavern. But he stepped in, and as he did this he rose to great size; he filled out the garments till they fitted; he was a giant, of Giant-Land. With the clothes came the wisdom, the m'teoulin, the manitou power of the greatest and wisest of the olden time. He was indeed Megumoowessoo, and had attained to the Mystery.

THE GRIZZLY PEOPLE

Along time ago, while smoke still curled from the smoke hole of the tepee, a great storm arose. The storm shook the tepee. Wind blew the smoke down the smoke hole. Old Man Above said to Little Daughter: "Climb up to the smoke hole. Tell Wind to be quiet. Stick your arm out of the smoke hole before you tell him." Little Daughter climbed up to the smoke hole and put out her arm. But Little Daughter put out her head also. She wanted to see the world. Little Daughter wanted to see the rivers and trees, and the white foam on the Bitter Waters. Wind caught Little Daughter by the hair. Wind pulled her out of the smoke hole and blew her down the mountain. Wind blew Little Daughter over the smooth ice and the great forests, down to the land of the Grizzlies. Wind tangled her hair and then left her cold and shivering near the tepees of the Grizzlies.

Soon Grizzly came home. In those days Grizzly walked on two feet, and carried a big stick. Grizzly could talk as people do. Grizzly laid down the young elk he had killed and picked up Little Daughter. He took Little Daughter to his tepee. Then Mother Grizzly warmed her by the fire. Mother Grizzly gave her food to eat.

Soon Little Daughter married the son of Grizzly. Their children were not Grizzlies. They were men. So the Grizzlies built a tepee for Little Daughter and her children. White men call the tepee Little Shasta.

At last Mother Grizzly sent a son to Old Man Above. Mother Grizzly knew that Little Daughter was the child of Old Man Above, but she was afraid. She said: "Tell Old Man Above that Little Daughter is alive."

Old Man Above climbed out of the smoke hole. He ran down the mountain side to the land of the Grizzlies. Old Man Above ran very quickly. Wherever he set his foot the snow melted. The snow melted very quickly and made streams of water. Now Grizzlies stood in line to welcome Old Man Above. They stood on two feet and carried clubs. Then Old Man Above saw his daughter and her children. He saw the new race of men. Then Old Man Above became very angry. He said to Grizzlies:

"Never speak again. Be silent. Neither shall ye stand upright. Ye shall use your hands as feet. Ye shall look downward."

Then Old Man Above put out the fire in the tepee. Smoke no longer curls from the smoke hole. He fastened the door of the tepee. The new race of men he drove out. Then Old Man Above took Little Daughter back to his tepee.

That is why grizzlies walk on four feet and look downward. Only when fighting they stand on two feet and use their fists like men.

(Shastika)

THE BOY AND THE BEAST

Once an old woman lived with her daughter and son-in-law and their little boy. They were following the trail of the Apache Indians. Now whenever a Pima Indian sees the trail of an Apache he draws a ring around it; then he can catch him sooner. And these Pimas drew circles around the trail of the Apaches they were following, but one night when they were asleep, the Apaches came down upon them. They took the man and younger woman by the hair and shook them out of their skins, just as one would shake corn out of a sack. So the boy and the old woman were left alone.

Now these two had to live on berries and anything they could find, and they wandered from place to place. In one place a strange beast, big enough to swallow people, camped in the bushes near them. The grand-mother told the boy not to go near these bushes. But the boy took some sharp stones in his hands, and went toward them. As he came near, the great monster began to breathe. He began to suck in his breath and he sucked the boy right into his stomach. But with his sharp stones the boy began to cut the beast, so that he died. Then the boy made a hole large enough to climb out of.

When his grandmother came to look for him, the boy met her and said, "I have killed that monster."

The grandmother said, "Oh, no. Such a little boy as you are to kill such a great monster!"

The boy said, "But I was inside of him, just look at the stones I cut him with."

Then the grandmother went softly up to the bushes, and looked at the monster. It was full of holes, just as the little boy had said.

Then they moved down among the berry bushes and had all they wanted to eat.

AGE OF MONSTERS

In this age of monsters, the country was again invaded by Oyahgua-harh, who was greater than the great mammoth. His fury was against men, and he destroyed the lives of many Indian hunters, but finally he was killed, after a long and severe battle.

Next, a great horned serpent appeared on Lake Ontario who, by means of his poisonous breath, caused disease, and many deaths. The old women of the tribe congregated, with one another, and prayed to the Great Spirit that he would send their grand-father, the Thunder, who would save them in their time of trouble. While praying they at the same time burned tobacco as an offering to the Thunder. Finally the monster was compelled to retreat in the depths of the lake by great thunder bolts. Before this calamity was forgotten another happened. A blazing star fell into the village, near the banks of the St. Lawrence, and destroyed the people. Such a phenomenon caused a great panic, consternation and dread, which they regarded as ominous of their entire destruction. These tribes, who were held together by feeble ties, fell into dispute and wars among themselves, which were pursued through a long period, until they had utterly destroyed each other, and so reduced their numbers that the lands were again over-run with wild beasts.

(Iroquois)

SPIRITS

THE FORKED ROADS

Long ago, in the days of the grandfathers, a man died and was buried by his village. For four nights his ghost had to walk a very dark trail. Then he reached the Milky Way and there was plenty of light. For this reason, people ought to keep the funeral fires lighted for four nights, so the spirit will not walk in the dark trail.

The spirit walked along the Milky Way. At last he came to a point where the trail forked. There sat an old man. He was dressed in a buffalo robe, with the hair on the outside. He pointed to each ghost the road he was to take. One was short and led to the land of good ghosts. The other was very long; along it the ghosts went wailing.

The spirits of suicides cannot travel either road. They must hover over their graves. For them there is no future life.

A murderer is never happy after he dies. Ghosts surround him and keep up a constant whistling. He is always hungry, though he eat much food. He is never allowed to go where he pleases, lest high winds arise and sweep down upon the others.

(Omaha)

TATTOOED GHOSTS

If a ghost wishes to walk the Ghost Road safely, then during living the person must tattoo himself either in the forehead or on the wrists. An old woman sits in the Ghost Road and she examines each ghost who passes. If she finds the tattoo marks, then the ghost travels on at once to Many Lodges. If the tattoo marks are not there, the old woman pushes the ghost from a cloud and he falls to this world again. Then he wanders all over the world. He is never quiet. He goes about whistling, with no lodge, and people are afraid of him.

When these ghosts visit the sick, they are driven away by smoke from the sacred cedar, or else cedar is laid outside the lodge. When a person hears a ghost whistling he goes outside the lodge and makes a loud noise. If a ghost calls to a loved one and he answers, then he is sure to die soon.

If a ghost meets a man who is alone, he will catch hold of him and pull his mouth and eyes until they are crooked. Indeed, a ghost did this to a person who only dreamed about one.

(Dakota)

A GHOST STORY

A great many persons went on the warpath. They were Ponca. As they approached the foe, they camped for the night. They kindled a fire. It was during the night. After kindling a bright fire, they sat down; they made the fire burn very brightly. Rejoicing greatly, they sat eating. Very suddenly a person sang.

"Keep quiet. Push the ashes over that fire. Seize your bow in silence!" said their leader. All took their bows. And they departed to surround him. They made the circle smaller and smaller, and commenced at once to come together. And still he stood singing; he did not stir at all. At length they went very near to the tree. And when they drew very near to it, the singer ceased his song. When they had reached the tree, bones lay there in a pile. Human bones were piled there at the foot of the tree. When persons die, the Dakotas usually suspend the bodies in trees.

(Ponca)

THE SPIRIT LAND

The spirit world is toward the Darkening Land, higher up, and separated from the world of living by a great lake. Now when the spirits came back to this world Crow was their leader. That is because Crow is black; his color is the same as that of the Darkening Land. Crow was followed by all the Indians. But when they reached the edge of the shadow land, below them was a great sea.

Far away, toward the Sunrise Land were their people in the world of living. So Crow took a pebble in his beak. He dropped it into the water, and it became a mountain, towering up to the shadow land. So the Indians came down the mountain side to the edge of the water.

Then Crow took some dust in his bill. He flew out and dropped it into the water, and it became solid land. It stretched between the spirit land and the world of living.

Then Crow flew out again, with blades of grass in his beak. He dropped these upon the new made land. At once the earth was covered with green grass.

Again Crow flew out with twigs in his beak, and he dropped these upon the new earth. At once it was covered with a forest of trees.

Again he flew back to the base of the mountain. Then he called all the spirit Indians together. Now he is coming to help the living Indians. He has already passed the sea. He is now on the western edge of the world of living.

(Arapahoe)

THE GHOST AND THE TRAVELER

Once an Indian alone was just at the edge of a forest. Then the Thunder Beings raised a great storm. So he remained there for the night. After it was dark, he noticed a light in the woods. When he reached the spot, behold! there was a sweat lodge, in which were two persons talking.

One said, "Friend, someone has come and stands without. Let us invite him to share our food."

Then the Indian fled because they were ghosts. But they followed him. He looked back now and then, but he could not see them.

All at once he heard the cry of a woman. He was glad to have company. But the moment he thought about the woman, she appeared. She said, "I have come because you have just wished to have company."

This frightened the man. The woman said, "Do not fear me; else you will never see me again."

They journeyed until daybreak. The man looked at her. She seemed to have no legs, yet she walked without any effort. Then the man thought, "What if she should choke me." Immediately the ghost vanished.

(Teton)

THE GIRL WHO MARRIED THE PINE-TREE

Upon the side of a certain mountain grew some pines, under the shade of which the Puckwudjinies were accustomed to sport at times. Now it happened that in the neighbourhood of these trees was a lodge in which dwelt a beautiful girl and her father and mother. One day a man came to the lodge of the father, and seeing the girl he loved her, and said—

"Give me Leelinau for my wife," and the old man consented.

Now it happened that the girl did not like her lover, so she escaped from the lodge and went and hid herself, and as the sun was setting she came to the pine-trees, and leaning against one of them she lamented her hard fate. Suddenly she heard a voice, which seemed to come from the tree, saying—

"Be my wife, maiden, beautiful Leelinau, beautiful Leelinau."

The girl was astonished, not knowing whence the voice could have come. She listened again, and the words were repeated, evidently by the tree against which she leaned. Then the maid consented to be the wife of the pine-tree.

Meanwhile her parents had missed her, and had sent out parties to see if she could be found, but she was nowhere.

Time passed on, but Leelinau never returned to her home. Hunters who have been crossing the mountain, and have come to the trees at sunset, say that they have seen a beautiful girl there in company with a handsome youth, who vanished as they approached.

THE MAN WHO SHOT A GHOST

In the olden time, a man was traveling alone, and in a forest he killed several rabbits. After sunset he was in the midst of the forest. He had to spend the night there, so he made a fire.

He thought this: "Should I meet any danger by and by, I will shoot. I am a man who ought not to regard anything."

He cooked a rabbit, so he was no longer hungry. Just then he heard many voices. They were talking about their own affairs. But the man could see no one.

So he thought: "It seems now that at last I have encountered ghosts."

Then he went and lay under a fallen tree, which was a great distance from the fire. They came around him and whistled, "*Hyu! hyu! hyu!*"

"He has gone yonder," said one of the ghosts. Then they came and stood around the man, just as people do when they hunt rabbits. The man lay flat beneath the fallen tree, and one ghost came and climbed on the trunk of that tree. Suddenly the ghost gave the cry that a man does when he hits an enemy, "*A-he!*" Then the ghost kicked the man in the back.

Before the ghost could get away, very suddenly the man shot at him and wounded him in the legs. So the ghost cried as men do in pain, "*Au! au! au!*" At last he went off, crying as women do, "*Yun! yun! yun! yun!*"

The other ghosts said to him, "Where did he shoot?"

The wounded ghost said, "He shot me through the head and I have come apart." The other ghosts began wailing on the hillside.

The man decided he would go to the place where the ghosts were moaning. So when day came, he went there and found their graves. One of them a wolf had dug, so that the bones could be seen; and there was a bullet wound in the skull.

(Teton)

THE CAMP OF THE GHOSTS

There was once a man who loved his wife dearly. After they had been married for a time they had a little boy. Some time after that the woman grew sick and did not get well. She was sick for a long time. The young man loved his wife so much that he did not wish to take a second woman. The woman grew worse and worse. Doctoring did not seem to do her any good. At last she died.

For a few days after this, the man used to take his baby on his back and travel out away from the camp, walking over the hills, crying and mourning. He felt badly, and he did not know what to do.

After a time he said to the little child, "My little boy, you will have to go and live with your grandmother. I shall go away and try to find your mother and bring her back."

He took the baby to his mother's lodge and asked her to take care of it and left it with her. Then he started away, not knowing where he was going nor what he should do.

When he left the camp, he travelled toward the Sand Hills. On the fourth night of his journeying he had a dream. He dreamed that he went into a little lodge in which was an old woman. This old woman said to him, "Why are you here, my son?"

The young man replied, "I am mourning day and night, crying all the while. My little son, who is the only one left me, also mourns."

"Well," asked the old woman, "for whom are you mourning?"

The young man answered, "I am mourning for my wife. She died some time ago. I am looking for her."

"Oh, I saw her," said the old woman; "she passed this way. I myself have no great power to help you, but over by that far butte beyond, lives another old woman. Go to her and she will give you power to continue your journey. You could not reach the place you are seeking without help. Beyond the next butte from her lodge you will find the camp of the ghosts."

The next morning the young man awoke and went on toward the next butte. It took him a long summer's day to get there, but he found there no lodge, so he lay down and slept. Again he dreamed. In his dream he saw a little lodge, and saw an old woman come to the door and heard her call to him. He went into the lodge, and she spoke to him.

"My son, you are very unhappy. I know why you have come this way. You are looking for your wife who is now in the ghost country. It is a very hard thing for you to get there. You may not be able to get your wife back, but I have great power and I will do for you all that I can. If you act as I advise, you may succeed."

Other wise words she spoke to him, telling him what he should do;

also she gave him a bundle of mysterious things which would help him on his journey.

She went on to say, "You stay here for a time and I will go over there to the ghosts' camp and try to bring back some of your relations who are there. If it is possible for me to bring them back, you may return there with them, but on the way you must shut your eyes. If you should open them and look about you, you would die. Then you would never come back. When you come to the camp you will pass by a big lodge and they will ask you, 'Where are you going and who told you to come here?' You must answer, 'My grandmother, who is standing out here with me, told me to come.' They will try to scare you; they will make fearful noises and you will see strange and terrible things, but do not be afraid."

The old woman went away, and after a time came back with one of the man's relations. He went with this relation to the ghosts' camp. When they came to the large lodge some one called out and asked the man what he was doing there, and he answered as the old woman had told him. As he passed on through the camp the ghosts tried to frighten him with many fearful sights and sounds, but he kept up a strong heart.

Presently he came to another lodge, and the man who owned it came out and spoke to him, asking where he was going. The young man said, "I am looking for my dead wife. I mourn for her so much that I cannot rest. My little boy too keeps crying for his mother. They have offered to give me other wives, but I do not want them. I want the one for whom I am searching."

The ghost said, "It is a fearful thing that you have come here; it is very likely that you will never go away. Never before has there been a person here."

The ghost asked him to come into his lodge, and he entered.

This chief ghost said to him, "You shall stay here for four nights and you shall see your wife, but you must be very careful or you will never go back. You will die here in this very place."

Then the chief ghost walked out of the lodge and shouted out for a feast, inviting the man's father-in-law and other relations who were in the camp to come and eat, saying, "Your son-in-law invites you to a feast," as if he meant that the son-in-law had died and become a ghost and arrived at the camp of the ghosts.

Now when these invited ghosts had reached the lodge they did not like to go in. They said to each other, "There is a person here"; it seemed as if they did not like the smell of a human being. The chief ghost burned sweet pine on the fire, which took away this smell, and then the ghosts came in and sat down.

The chief ghost said to them, "Now pity this son-in-law of yours. He is looking for his wife. Neither the great distance that he has come nor the fearful sights that he has seen here have weakened his heart. You can see how tender-hearted he is. He not only mourns because he has lost his wife, but he mourns because his little boy is now alone, with no mother; so pity him and give him back his wife."

The ghosts talked among themselves, and one of them said to the man, "Yes; you shall stay here for four nights, and then we will give you a medicine pipe—the Worm Pipe—and we will give you back your wife and you may return to your home."

Now, after the third night the chief ghost called together all the people, and they came, and with them came the man's wife. One of the ghosts was beating a drum, and following him was another who carried the Worm Pipe, which they gave to him.

Then the chief ghost said, "Now be very careful; to-morrow you and your wife will start on your journey homeward. Your wife will carry the medicine pipe and for four days some of your relations will go along with you. During this time you must keep your eyes shut; do not open them, or you will return here and be a ghost forever. Your wife is not now a person. But in the middle of the fourth day you will be told to look, and when you have opened your eyes you will see that your wife has become a person, and that your ghost relations have disappeared."

Before the man went away his father-in-law spoke to him and said, "When you get near home you must not go at once into the camp. Let some of your relations know that you have come, and ask them to build a sweat-house for you. Go into that sweat-house and wash your body thoroughly, leaving no part of it, however small, uncleansed. If you fail in this, you will die. There is something about the ghosts that it is difficult to remove. It can only be removed by a thorough sweat. Take care now that you do what I tell you. Do not whip your wife, nor strike her with a knife, nor hit her with fire. If you do, she will vanish before your eyes and return here."

They left the ghost country to go home, and on the fourth day the wife said to her husband, "Open your eyes." He looked about him and saw that those who had been with them had disappeared, and he found that they were standing in front of the old woman's lodge by the butte. She came out of her lodge and said to them, "Stop; give me back those mysterious medicines of mine, whose power helped you to do what you wished." The man returned them to her, and then once more became really a living person.

When they drew near to the camp the woman went on ahead and sat down on a butte. Then some curious persons came out to see who this might be. As they approached the woman called out to them, "Do not come any nearer. Go and tell my mother and my relations to put up a lodge for us a little way from the camp, and near by it build a sweat-house." When this had been done the man and his wife went in and took a thorough sweat, and then they went into the lodge and burned sweet grass and purified their clothing and the Worm Pipe. Then their relations and friends came in to see them. The man told them where he had been and how he had managed to get his wife back, and that the pipe hanging over the doorway was a medicine pipe—the Worm Pipe—presented to him by his ghost father-in-law.

That is how the people came to possess the Worm Pipe. That pipe belongs to the band of Piegans known as the Worm People.

Not long after this, once in the night, this man told his wife to do something, and when she did not begin at once he picked up a brand from the fire and raised it—not that he intended to strike her with it, but he made as if he would—when all at once she vanished and was never seen again.

THE INDIAN WHO WRESTLED WITH A GHOST

A young man went alone on the warpath. At length he reached a wood. One day, as he was going along, he heard a voice. He said, "I shall have company." As he was approaching a forest, he heard some one halloo. Behold, it was an owl.

By and by he drew near another wood, and as night was coming on he lay down to rest. At the edge of the trees he lay down in the open air. At midnight he was aroused by the voice of a woman. She was wailing, "My son! my son!" Still he remained where he was, and put more wood on the fire. He lay with his back to the fire. He tore a hole in his blanket large enough to peep through.

Soon he heard twigs break under the feet of one approaching, so he looked through his blanket without rising. Behold, a woman of the olden days was coming. She wore a skin dress with long fringe. A buffalo robe was fastened around her at the waist. Her necklace was of very large beads, and her leggings were covered with beads or porcupine work. Her robe was drawn over her head and she was snuffing as she came.

The man lay with his legs stretched out, and she stood by him. She took him by one foot, which she raised very slowly. When she let it go, it fell with a thud as though he were dead. She raised it a second time; then a third time. Still the man did not move. Then the woman pulled a very rusty knife from the front of her belt, seized his foot suddenly and was about to lift it and cut it, when up sprang the man. He said, "What are you doing?" Then he shot at her suddenly. She ran into the forest screaming, "*Yun! yun! yun! yun! yun! yun!*" She plunged into the forest and was seen no more.

Again the man covered his head with his blanket but he did not sleep. When day came, he raised his eyes. Behold, there was a burial scaffold, with the blankets all ragged and dangling. He thought, "Was this the ghost that came to me?"

Again he came to a wood where he had to remain for the night. He started a fire. As he sat there, suddenly he heard someone singing. He made the woods ring. The man shouted to the singer, but no answer was paid. The man had a small quantity of *wasna*, which was grease mixed with pounded buffalo meat, and wild cherry; he also had plenty of tobacco.

So when the singer came and asked him for food, the man said, "I have nothing." The ghost said, "Not so; I know you have some *wasna.*"

Then the man gave some of it to the ghost and filled his pipe. After the meal, when the stranger took the pipe and held it by the stem, the traveler saw that it was nothing but bones. There was no flesh. Then the stranger's robe dropped back from his shoulders. Behold, all his ribs were visible. There was no flesh on them. The ghost did not open his lips when he smoked. The smoke came pouring out through his ribs.

When he had finished smoking, the ghost said, "Ho! we must wrestle together. If you can throw me, you shall kill the enemy without hindrance and steal some horses."

The young man agreed. But first he threw an armful of brush on the fire. He put plenty of brush near the fire.

Then the ghost rushed at the man. He seized him with his bony hands, which was very painful; but this mattered not. The man tried to push off the ghost, whose legs were very powerful. When the ghost was pulled near the fire, he became weak; but when he pulled the young man toward the darkness, he became strong. As the fire got low, the strength of the ghost increased. Just as the man began to get weary, the day broke. Then the struggle began again. As they drew near the fire again, the man made a last effort; with his foot he pushed more brush into the fire. The fire blazed up again suddenly. Then the ghost fell, just as if he was coming to pieces.

So the man won in wrestling. Also he killed his enemy and stole some horses. It came out just as the ghost said. That is why people believe what ghosts say.

(Teton)

HEAVY COLLAR AND THE GHOST WOMAN

The Blood camp was on Old Man's River, where Fort McLeod now stands. A party of seven men started to war toward the Cypress Hills. Heavy Collar was the leader. They went around the Cypress Mountains, but found no enemies and started back toward their camp. On their homeward way, Heavy Collar used to take the lead. He would go out far ahead on the high hills, and look over the country, acting as scout for the party. At length they came to the south branch of the Saskatchewan River, above Seven Persons' Creek. In those days there were many war parties about, and this party travelled concealed as much as possible in the coulées and low places.

As they were following up the river, they saw at a distance three old bulls lying down close to a cut bank. Heavy Collar left his party, and went out to kill one of these bulls, and when he had come close to them, he shot one and killed it right there. He cut it up, and, as he was hungry, he went down into a ravine below him, to roast a piece of meat; for he had left his party a long way behind, and night was now coming on. As he was roasting the meat, he thought,—for he was very tired,—"It is a pity I did not bring one of my young men with me. He could go up on that hill and get some hair from that bull's head, and I could wipe out my gun." While he sat there thinking this, and talking to himself, a bunch of this hair came over him through the air, and fell on the ground right in front of him. When this happened, it frightened him a little; for he thought that perhaps some of his enemies were close by, and had thrown the bunch of hair at him. After a little while, he took the hair, and cleaned his gun and loaded it, and then sat and watched for a time. He was uneasy, and at length decided that he would go on further up the river, to see what he could discover. He went on, up the stream, until he came to the mouth of the St. Mary's River. It was now very late in the night, and he was very tired, so he crept into a large bunch of rye-grass to hide and sleep for the night.

The summer before this, the Blackfeet (Sik-si-kau) had been camped on this bottom, and a woman had been killed in this same patch of rye-grass where Heavy Collar had lain down to rest. He did not know this, but still he seemed to be troubled that night. He could not sleep. He could always hear something, but what it was he could not make out. He tried to go to sleep, but as soon as he dozed off he kept thinking he heard something in the distance. He spent the night there, and in the morning when it became light, there he saw right beside him the skeleton of the woman who had been killed the summer before.

That morning he went on, following up the stream to Belly River. All day long as he was travelling, he kept thinking about his having slept by this woman's bones. It troubled him. He could not forget it. At the same time he was very tired, because he had walked so far and had slept so little. As night came on, he crossed over to an island, and determined to camp for the night. At the upper end of the island was a large tree that had drifted down and lodged, and in a fork of this tree he built his fire, and got in a crotch of one of the forks, and sat with his back to the fire, warming himself, but all the time he was thinking about the woman he had slept beside the night before. As he sat there, all at once he heard over beyond the tree, on the other side of the fire, a sound as if something were being dragged toward him along the ground. It sounded as if a piece of a lodge were being dragged over the grass. It came closer and closer.

Heavy Collar was scared. He was afraid to turn his head and look back to see what it was that was coming. He heard the noise come up to the tree in which his fire was built, and then it stopped, and all at once he heard some one whistling a tune. He turned around and looked toward the sound, and there, sitting on the other fork of the tree, right opposite to him, was the pile of bones by which he had slept, only now all together in the shape of a skeleton. This ghost had on it a lodge covering. The string, which is tied to the pole, was fastened about the ghost's neck; the wings of the lodge stood out on either side of its head, and behind it the lodge could be seen, stretched out and fading away into the darkness. The ghost sat on the old dead limb and whistled its tune, and as it whistled, it swung its legs in time to the tune.

When Heavy Collar saw this, his heart almost melted away. At length he mustered up courage, and said: "Oh ghost, go away, and do not trouble me. I am very tired; I want to rest." The ghost paid no attention to him, but kept on whistling, swinging its legs in time to the tune. Four times he prayed to her, saying: "Oh ghost, take pity on me! Go away and leave me alone. I am tired; I want to rest." The more he prayed, the more the ghost whistled and seemed pleased, swinging her legs, and turning her head from side to side, sometimes looking down at him, and sometimes up at the stars, and all the time whistling.

When he saw that she took no notice of what he said, Heavy Collar got angry at heart, and said, "Well, ghost, you do not listen to my prayers, and I shall have to shoot you to drive you away." With that he seized his gun, and throwing it to his shoulder, shot right at the ghost. When he shot at her, she fell over backward into the darkness, screaming out: "Oh Heavy Collar, you have shot me, you have killed me! You dog, Heavy Collar! there is no place on this earth where you can go that I will not find you; no place where you can hide that I will not come."

As she fell back and said this, Heavy Collar sprang to his feet, and ran away as fast as he could. She called after him: "I have been killed once, and now you are trying to kill me again. Oh Heavy Collar!" As he ran away, he could still hear her angry words following him, until at last they died away in the distance. He ran all night long, and whenever he stopped to breathe and listen, he seemed to hear in the distance the echoes of her voice. All he could hear was, "Oh Heavy Collar!" and then he would rush away again. He ran until he was all tired out, and by this time it was daylight. He was now quite a long way below Fort McLeod. He was very sleepy, but dared not lie down, for he remembered that the ghost had said that she would follow him. He kept walking on for some time, and then sat down to rest, and at once fell asleep.

Before he had left his party, Heavy Collar had said to his young men: "Now remember, if any one of us should get separated from the party, let him always travel to the Belly River Buttes. There will be our meeting-place." When their leader did not return to them, the party started across the country and went toward the Belly River Buttes. Heavy Collar had followed the river up, and had gone a long distance out of his way; and when he awoke from his sleep he too started straight for the Belly River Buttes, as he had said he would.

When his party reached the Buttes, one of them went up on top of the hill to watch. After a time, as he looked down the river, he saw two persons coming, and as they came nearer, he saw that one of them was Heavy Collar, and by his side was a woman. The watcher called up the rest of the party, and said to them: "Here comes our chief. He has had luck. He is bringing a woman with him. If he brings her into camp, we will take her away from him." And they all laughed. They supposed that he had captured her. They went down to the camp, and sat about the fire, looking at the two people coming, and laughing among themselves at the idea of their chief bringing in a woman. When the two persons had come close, they could see that

Heavy Collar was walking fast, and the woman would walk by his side a little way, trying to keep up, and then would fall behind, and then trot along to catch up to him again. Just before the pair reached camp there was a deep ravine that they had to cross. They went down into this side by side, and then Heavy Collar came up out of it alone, and came on into the camp.

When he got there, all the young men began to laugh at him and to call out, "Heavy Collar, where is your woman?" He looked at them for a moment, and then said: "Why, I have no woman. I do not understand what you are talking about." One of them said: "Oh, he has hidden her in that ravine. He was afraid to bring her into camp." Another said, "Where did you capture her, and what tribe does she belong to?" Heavy Collar looked from one to another, and said: "I think you are all crazy. I have taken no woman. What do you mean?" The young man said: "Why, that woman that you had with you just now: where did you get her, and where did you leave her? Is she down in the coulée? We all saw her, and it is no use to deny that she was with you. Come now, where is she?" When they said this, Heavy Collar's heart grew very heavy, for he knew that it must have been the ghost woman; and he told them the story. Some of the young men could not believe this, and they ran down to the ravine, where they had last seen the woman. There they saw in the soft dirt the tracks made by Heavy Collar, when he went down into the ravine, but there were no other tracks near his, where they had seen the woman walking. When they found that it was a ghost that had come along with Heavy Collar, they resolved to go back to their main camp. The party had been out so long that their moccasins were all worn out, and some of them were footsore, so that they could not travel fast, but at last they came to the cut banks, and there found their camp—seven lodges.

That night, after they had reached camp, they were inviting each other to feasts. It was getting pretty late in the night, and the moon was shining brightly, when one of the Bloods called out for Heavy Collar to come and eat with him. Heavy Collar shouted, "Yes, I will be there pretty soon." He got up and went out of the lodge, and went a little way from it, and sat down. While he was sitting there, a big bear walked out of the brush close to him. Heavy Collar felt around him for a stone to throw at the bear, so as to scare it away, for he thought it had not seen him. As he was feeling about, his hand came upon a piece of bone, and he threw this over at the bear, and hit it. Then the bear spoke, and said: "Well, well, well, Heavy Collar; you have killed me once, and now here you are hitting me. Where is there a place in this world where you can hide from me? I will find you, I don't care where you may go." When Heavy Collar heard this, he knew it was the ghost woman, and he jumped up and ran toward his lodge, calling out, "Run, run! a ghost bear is upon us!"

All the people in the camp ran to his lodge, so that it was crowded full of people. There was a big fire in the lodge, and the wind was blowing hard from the west. Men, women, and children were huddled together in the lodge, and were very much afraid of the ghost. They could hear her walking toward the lodge, grumbling, and saying: "I will kill all these dogs. Not one of them shall get away." The sounds kept coming closer and closer, until they were right at the lodge door. Then she said, "I will smoke you to death." And as she said this, she moved the poles, so that the wings of the lodge turned toward the west, and the wind could blow in freely through the smoke hole. All this time she was threatening terrible things against them. The lodge began to get full of smoke, and the children were crying, and all were in great distress—almost suffocating. So they said, "Let us lift one man up here inside, and let him try to fix the ears, so that the lodge will get clear of smoke." They raised a man up, and he was standing on the shoulders of the others, and, blinded and half strangled by the smoke, was trying to turn the wings. While he was doing this, the ghost suddenly hit the lodge a blow, and said, "Un!" and this scared the people who were holding the man, and they jumped and let him go, and he fell down. Then the people were in despair, and said, "It is no use; she is resolved to smoke us to death." All the time the smoke was getting thicker in the lodge.

Heavy Collar said: "Is it possible that she can destroy us? Is there no one here who has some strong dream power that can overcome this ghost?"

His mother said: "I will try to do something. I am older than any of you, and I will see what I can do." So she got down her medicine bundle and painted herself, and got out a pipe and filled it and lighted it, and stuck the stem out through the lodge door, and sat there and began to pray to the ghost woman. She said: "Oh ghost, take pity on us, and go away. We have never wronged you, but you are troubling us and frightening our children. Accept what I offer you, and leave us alone."

A voice came from behind the lodge and said: "No, no, no; you dogs, I will not listen to you. Every one of you must die."

The old woman repeated her prayer: "Ghost, take pity on us. Accept this smoke and go away."

Then the ghost said: "How can you expect me to smoke, when I am way back here? Bring that pipe out here. I have no long bill to reach round the lodge." So the old woman went out of the lodge door, and reached out the stem of the pipe as far as she could reach around toward the back of the lodge. The ghost said: "No, I do not wish to go around there to where you have that pipe. If you want me to smoke it, you must bring it here." The old woman went around the lodge toward her, and the ghost woman began to back away, and said, "No, I do not smoke that kind of a pipe." And when the ghost started away, the old woman followed her, and she could not help herself.

She called out, "Oh my children, the ghost is carrying me off!" Heavy Collar rushed out, and called to the others, "Come, and help me take my mother from the ghost." He grasped his mother about the waist and held her, and another man took him by the waist, and another him, until they were all strung out, one behind the other, and all following the old woman, who was following the ghost woman, who was walking away.

All at once the old woman let go of the pipe, and fell over dead. The ghost disappeared, and they were troubled no more by the ghost woman.

(Blackfoot)

THE JEEBI

There lived a hunter in the north who had a wife and one child. His lodge stood far off in the forest, several days' journey from any other. He spent his days in hunting, and his evenings in relating to his wife the incidents that had befallen him. As game was very abundant, he found no difficulty in killing as much as they wanted. Just in all his acts, he lived a peaceful and happy life.

One evening during the winter season, it chanced that he remained out later than usual, and his wife began to feel uneasy, for fear some accident had befallen him. It was already dark. She listened attentively, and at last heard the sound of approaching footsteps. Not doubting it was her husband, she went to the door and beheld two strange females. She bade them enter, and invited them to remain.

She observed that they were total strangers in the country. There was something so peculiar in their looks, air, and manner, that she was uneasy in their company. They would not come near the fire; they sat in a remote part of the lodge, were shy and taciturn, and drew their garments about them in such a manner as nearly to hide their faces. So far as she could judge, they were pale, hollow-eyed, and long-visaged, very thin and emaciated. There was but little light in the lodge, as the fire was low, and served by its fitful flashes, rather to increase than dispel their fears. "Merciful spirit!" cried a voice from the opposite part of the lodge, "there are two corpses clothed with garments." The hunter's wife turned around, but seeing nobody, she concluded the sounds were but gusts of wind. She trembled, and was ready to sink to the earth.

Her husband at this moment entered and dispelled her fears. He threw down the carcass of a large fat deer. "Behold what a fine and fat animal," cried the mysterious females, and they immediately ran and pulled off pieces of the whitest fat, which they ate with greediness. The hunter and his wife looked on with astonishment, but remained silent. They supposed their guests might have been famished. Next day, however, the same unusual conduct was repeated. The strange females tore off the fat and devoured it with eagerness. The third day the hunter thought he would anticipate their wants by tying up a portion of the fattest pieces for them, which he placed on the top of his load. They accepted it, but still appeared dissatisfied, and went to the wife's portion and tore off more. The man and his wife felt surprised at such rude and unaccountable conduct, but they remained silent, for they respected their guests, and had observed that they had been attended with marked good luck during the residence of these mysterious visitors.

In other respects, the deportment of the females was strictly unexceptionable. They were modest, distant, and silent. They never uttered a word during the day. At night they would occupy themselves in procuring wood, which they carried to the lodge, and then returning the implements exactly to the places in which they had found them, resume their places without speaking. They were never known to stay out until daylight. They never laughed or jested.

The winter had nearly passed away, without anything uncommon happening, when, one evening, the hunter stayed out very late. The moment he entered and laid down his day's hunt as usual before his wife, the two females began to tear off the fat, in so unceremonious a way, that her anger was excited. She constrained herself, however, in a measure, but did not conceal her feelings, although she said but little. The guests observed the excited state of her mind, and became unusually reserved and uneasy. The good hunter saw the change, and carefully inquired into the cause, but his wife denied having used any hard words. They retired to their couches, and he tried to compose himself to sleep, but could not, for the sobs and sighs of the two females were incessant. He arose on his couch and addressed them as follows:—

"Tell me," said he, "what is it that gives you pain of mind, and causes you to utter those sighs. Has my wife given you offence, or trespassed on the rights of hospitality?"

They replied in the negative. "We have been treated by you with kindness and affection. It is not for any slight we have received that we weep. Our mission is not to you only. We come from the land of the dead to test mankind, and to try the sincerity of the living. Often we have heard the bereaved by death say that if the dead could be restored, they would devote their lives to make them happy. We have been moved by the bitter lamentations which have reached the place of the dead, and have come to make proof of the sincerity of those who have lost friends. Three moons were allotted us by the Master of Life to make the trial. More than half the time had been successfully past, when the angry feelings of your wife indicated the irksomeness you felt at our presence, and has made us resolve on our departure."

They continued to talk to the hunter and his wife, gave them instructions as to a future life, and pronounced a blessing upon them.

"There is one point," they added, "of which we wish to speak. You have thought our conduct very strange in rudely possessing ourselves of the choicest parts of your hunt. That was the point of trial selected to put you to. It is the wife's peculiar privilege. For another to usurp it, we knew to be the severest trial of her, and consequently of your temper and feelings. We know your manners and customs, but we came to prove you, not by a compliance with them, but a violation of them. Pardon us. We are the agents of him who sent us. Peace to your dwelling, adieu!"

When they ceased, total darkness filled the lodge. No object could be seen. The inmates heard the door open and shut, but they never saw more of the two Jeebi-ug.

The hunter found the success which they had promised. He became celebrated in the chase, and never wanted for anything. He had many children, all of whom grew up to manhood, and health; peace, and long life were the rewards of his hospitality.

(Ojibwa)

Barechested Navajo man dressed as the benevolent female deity Haschebaad.

Bibliography and Futher Reading

Blackbird, Andrew J.:
History of the Ottawa and Chippewa Indians of Michigan - Michigan, 1887
Gibbins, W.W.:
Folk-Lore And Legends North American Indian - London, W.C., 1890
Grinnell, George Bird:
Blackfoot Lodge Tales, Year Unknown
Jones, James Athearn:
Traditions Of The North American Indians - London, Year Unknown
Judson, Katharine Berry:
Myths And Legends Of California And The Old Southwest, Year Unknown
Judson, Katharine Berry:
Myths And Legends Of The Great Plains - Chicago, 1913
Leland, Charles G.:
The Algonquin Legends Of New England, Year Unknown
Linderman, Frank B.:
Indian Why Stories. Sparks From War Eagle's Lodge-Fire, Year Unknown
Mathews, Cornelius:
The Indian Fairy Book - New York: Allen Brothers, 1869
Powers, Mabel:
Stories The Iroquois Tell Their Children - New York, 1917
Severance, Cordenio A.:
Indian Legends Of Minnesota - New York: D. D. Merrill Compan, 1893
Spence, Lewis:
Myths and Legends of the North American Indians - 1914
Zitkala-Sa:
Old Indian Legends, Year Unknown

Various Words & Meanings

The words presented below have multiple spelling variations which are have not been presented due to a lack of required space. The words were selected to give an example of the descriptive and inventive nature of the speaker's languages.

Ahnunggokwan: Star World (Ojibwe)

Animikii: Thunder Bird (Anishinabe)

Catsina: Human Spirit (Hopi)

D-li': Bluebird, the representative of peace (Navajo)

Gitchie Manito: Great Mystery (Ojibwe)

Hotsko: Wise Owl (Hopi)

ishałde'ma: Eternity (Zuni)

Keelut: Evil Spirit in the form of a dog (Inuit)

Kwasinabóo: Snake or Serpent (Comanche)

Maeci-Kenupik: Great Underwater Serpent (Menominee)

Neegawnnakayg: Prophets (Ojibwe)

Nunnehi: Traveler Spirits (Cherokee)

Pawgwa-tchaw-nishnawboy: Wild supernatural being (Chippewa)

Tibik-kìzis: The Moon (Algonquin)

Uktena: Horned Dragon Serpent (Cherokee)

Wakan: Mysterious (Lakota)

Windigo: Evil man-eating spirit (Anishinabe)

Yontare: Lake or Great Lake (Huron)

Yunwi Tsunsdi': Nature Spirits (Cherokee)

About John E.L. Tenney

John E.L. Tenney lives in a small suburb of Detroit, Michigan.
He has been actively involved in the research and investigation
of anomalistic phenomena and folkloric traditions since 1986.

For more information email:

john@weirdlectures.com